CITYSPOTS
DÜSSELDORF

WHAT'S IN YOUR GUIDEBOOK?

Independent authors Impartial up-to-date information from our travel experts who meticulously source local knowledge.

Experience Thomas Cook's 165 years in the travel industry and guidebook publishing enriches every word with expertise you can trust.

Travel know-how Contributions by thousands of staff around the globe, each one living and breathing travel.

Editors Travel-publishing professionals, pulling everything together to craft a perfect blend of words, pictures, maps and design.

You, the traveller We deliver a practical, no-nonsense approach to information, geared to how you really use it.

CITYSPOTS
DÜSSELDORF

Ryan Levitt

Thomas Cook

Written by Ryan Levitt
Original photography by Christopher Holt
Front cover photography (Frank Gehry's Neuer Zollhof) © Werner Dieterich/
Getty Images
Series design based on an original concept by Studio 183 Limited

Produced by Cambridge Publishing Management Limited
Project Editor: Penny Isaac
Layout: Trevor Double
Maps: PC Graphics
Transport map: © Communicarta Limited

Published by Thomas Cook Publishing
A division of Thomas Cook Tour Operations Limited
Company Registration No. 1450464 England
PO Box 227, Unit 18, Coningsby Road
Peterborough PE3 8SB, United Kingdom
email: books@thomascook.com
www.thomascookpublishing.com
+ 44 (0) 1733 416477
ISBN: 978-1-84157-757-9

First edition © 2007 Thomas Cook Publishing
Text © 2007 Thomas Cook Publishing
Maps © 2007 Thomas Cook Publishing
Project Editor: Kelly Anne Pipes
Production/DTP: Steven Collins

Printed and bound in Spain by GraphyCems

All rights reserved. No part of this publication may be reproduced, stored in
a retrieval system or transmitted, in any form or by any means, electronic,
mechanical, recording or otherwise, in any part of the world, without prior
permission of the publisher. Requests for permission should be made to the
publisher at the above address.

Although every care has been taken in compiling this publication, and the contents
are believed to be correct at the time of printing, Thomas Cook Tour Operations
Limited cannot accept any responsibility for errors or omission, however caused,
or for changes in details given in the guidebook, or for the consequences of any
reliance on the information provided. Descriptions and assessments are based on
the author's views and experiences when writing and do not necessarily represent
those of Thomas Cook Tour Operations Limited.

CONTENTS

SYMBOLS KEY

The following symbols are used throughout this book:

@ address ☎ telephone 🌐 website address
🕐 opening times 🚍 public transport connections

The following symbols are used on the maps:

𝒊	information office	O	city
🛫	airport	O	large town
✚	hospital	○	small town
🛡	police station	▪	poi (point of interest)
🚌	bus station	=	motorway
🚆	railway station	—	main road
Ⓤ	U-Bahn	—	minor road
✝	church	—	railway
❶	numbers denote featured cafés & restaurants		

Hotels and restaurants are graded by approximate price as follows:

£ budget ££ mid-range £££ expensive

▶ Düsseldorf's dreaming spires

Introduction

Düsseldorf has never been on the 'must-see' list for holidaymakers travelling to Germany. For years, visitors have avoided this European metropolis in favour of the more historically intriguing cultural trappings of nearby Cologne (Köln). Sure, many have passed by Düsseldorf on a Rhine river cruise, but few get off to explore its sights – and for that they should be severely rebuked.

To miss Düsseldorf is to miss one of Germany's most cosmopolitan cities. There's money in these streets, thanks in large part to the numerous multinationals, advertising agencies, media moguls and manufacturers who base themselves here. And with money come great fashion, architecture and design.

Residents of Düsseldorf battle it out with the citizens of Hamburg and Munich for the title of the richest in Germany. What they don't battle over, however, is the war over chic and sophistication. Everyone knows that when it comes to clothes and interiors, a Düsseldorfer will always win.

A break in Düsseldorf is rewarding. Not only will locals go out of their way to make sure you have a good time, you'll find that the museums and sights in the region are relatively undiscovered. What does this mean? No endless queuing, fantastic restaurants and streets that aren't filled with tourists opening their maps on every corner. This doesn't mean the city isn't worth visiting, it's just that the vast majority of travellers have yet to uncover the possibilities of this amazing style Mecca.

For shopping, Düsseldorf quite simply cannot be beaten. Almost every major designer has a boutique within the city limits. And if they don't, then they aren't worth buying. At least, that's what a local thinks.

Spend your days exploring the cobbled lanes of Altstadt (Old Town) and your nights hanging with the hip in Medienhafen. A better time you'll never have.

🔺 *Striking design is part of the exciting mix in Düsseldorf*

When to go

As Düsseldorf is one of Germany's biggest cities, you can be pretty sure that something will be going on there almost every week of the year. The city is highly focused on business travel, and you will experience less crowding during the traditional peak summer season – making this the best time to plan a visit. Winter has its own pleasures in the form of the annual Karneval (see page 14) that kicks off in November and lasts almost the entire season. Expect partying hordes in the main squares during this time of the year. Make your holiday special by dressing up and joining the throngs as they down their beers and sing traditional songs. While you may not know the words, you'll still receive a warm welcome.

SEASONS & CLIMATE

Düsseldorf's climate is like much of the rest of the nation – hot in summer and cold in winter. While Hamburg gets the winds from the Baltic, and Berlin can have freezing blasts that cut across from Eastern Europe, Düsseldorf benefits from a relatively unexposed position on the banks of the Rhine. Chilly breezes can sweep across this mighty river from time to time, but extremes are rare. In January and February, the city often ices over, with spring thawing everything out some time in late March or early April. Around this time, temperatures warm up enough to allow outdoor activities such as walking and cycling.

Summers can be hot and muggy, and at this time of the year locals flee to their country retreats or go boating on the river. In early autumn, temperatures are still very mild and, as in spring,

◆ *Capture the Christmas spirit in the fabulous markets*

this is a good time to explore the city's surroundings either on foot or by bicycle. In winter, sudden snowstorms occasionally occur. Wrap up warm, and join the partying Karneval throngs to banish your blues (see page 14).

ANNUAL EVENTS

In Düsseldorf and the North Rhine-Westphalia region, there are a huge range of events; the tourist offices in Düsseldorf and the surrounding region can provide a full list . Also note that exact dates may change from year to year – check first. There is a comprehensive calendar of events at
Ⓦ www.duesseldorf-tourismus.de

June
Düsseldorfer Jazz Rally Germany's largest celebration of jazz music hits town every year for three days in late June. It has been a feature of the Düsseldorf calendar for 15 years. Thousands of music fans congregate in the city for over 80 concerts in venues all over Düsseldorf. Expect names big and small, local and international. Book your hotel well in advance if you want to enjoy the sweet sounds.

July
The Sankt-Sebastianus Festival The biggest funfair on the Rhine hits the city every year on 11 July for nine days to celebrate the local marksmen's guild. Dating back to 1316, the festival attracts over 4.5 million visitors to the 300-plus stands on the Rhine meadows at Oberkassel. A massive fireworks display on the last day ends everything with a bang.

November

St Martin's Evening This local holiday held annually on
10 November celebrates the story of a Roman legionary who
once shared his coat with a cold beggar. Children create
homemade lanterns and parade through the streets at
nightfall, ending with the 'sharing of the coat' re-enactment
in front of the town hall. A traditional meal of roast goose
accompanies the evening treats.

December

Christmas markets The Altstadt and Schadowplatz fill with the
smell of mulled wine, the sight of twinkling lights and
ornaments, and the sound of laughter as the famous Christmas
market comes to town. Pull out your wallet and prepare for
some enjoyable Christmas shopping.

PUBLIC HOLIDAYS
New Year's Day 1 January
Good Friday March/April
Easter Monday March/April
Labour Day 1 May
Whit Monday May/June
Corpus Christi June
Day of Unity 3 October
All Saints' Day 1 November
Christmas Day 25 December
Boxing Day 26 December

Karneval

The residents of Düsseldorf have a reputation for conservatism and can be seen as aloof. All of this is banished, however, when Karneval celebrations hit the city. The fun begins at 11.11 on 11 November and continues until the arrival of Lent – usually in February.

Düsseldorf's reputation for celebration stems largely from the fact that the city is situated in a major wine-producing region. Where alcohol is produced, party-goers follow – Catholic and Protestant, local and travelling.

The tradition of celebrating Karneval dates back to pre-Christian times when the Germanic tribes tried to banish the ghosts of winter darkness until the arrival of spring. Many historians see the final procession – known as *Rosenmontagszug* (Rose Monday) – as both a last attempt to banish evil spirits and a first welcome to the Goddess Freya, known before the arrival of organised religion as the Goddess of Spring.

While 11 November is the first official day of Karneval season, it is far from its most important. On this day, various parade princes and princesses are selected and the town hall is stormed in order for the mayor to hand over the keys to the city.

The real fun begins on 6 January when the processions and parties begin to heat up. On almost every weekend from this date until Lent, there will be celebrations going on.

Finally there is the procession. Always held on Rose Monday (six weeks before Easter), the procession is packed with masked paraders, decorated trucks, bands and fuelled by lots of alcohol.

Expect over 1 million people to join in the fun, and prepare to join a conga line that will snake through the city until well after the sun has set.

○ Clowning around at Karneval

History

The city of Düsseldorf was first mentioned in written records in 1135. However, Germanic tribes had been living on the banks of the Rhine as far back as the 7th century. With an economy based mostly on small-scale farming and fishing, the region wasn't considered very important until the Emperor Friedrich Barbarossa built a fortified outpost in the town of Kaiserswerth, just to the north of today's city centre.

The Counts of Berg moved the seat of power to the town in 1280, with formal city status granted eight years later. The declaration was given following a civil war between the Archbishop of Cologne and the Count of Berg, which wiped out the archbishop's forces and elevated Düsseldorf's importance as a city of trade and power. To this day, citizens of the two cities dislike each other – a fact that wasn't helped by the massive economic boom experienced by Düsseldorf during the later years of the Industrial Revolution. Cologne didn't experience as much prosperity, and tensions grew as a result.

In 1380, Düsseldorf increased in importance yet again after it was declared the regional capital. From this moment on, the city drew the best and brightest artists, architects, merchants and writers. Several of the city's most famous landmarks were built during this period, including much of the original buildings of the Altstadt, although most were rebuilt in their original style following World War II.

The greatest leader of Düsseldorf is thought to be Johann Wilhelm II, also known as Jan Wellem, who ruled for just over a quarter of a century in the late 17th and early 18th centuries.

This art aficionado built up a massive collection of treasures and housed them in the city castle. Following his death, the city declined: the ruling Elector, Karl Theodor, inherited the much more attractive region of Bavaria and quickly moved the royal court to Munich. With him went the art collection lovingly pieced together by Johann Wilhelm II – never to return.

The Industrial Revolution returned Düsseldorf to its former glory – the city's position on the Rhine and its links to almost all of the major European trainlines made it an extremely attractive base. The population boomed to 100,000 – doubling to 200,000 just a decade later.

Düsseldorf's status as an industrial city proved to be its downfall during both World Wars I and II. Air raids destroyed the city, but reconstruction followed. Today, Düsseldorf is considered one of the richest cities in Germany.

● *The Rhine played a crucial role in the city's history and development*

Lifestyle

With one of the highest standards of living in Germany, the city of Düsseldorf offers an enviable lifestyle – and don't its residents know it. Chic boutiques, a remodelled and easy-to-navigate city centre, sophisticated restaurants and cultural institutions all come together to give the metropolis an international flavour. That, combined with a large ex-pat community, a plethora of multinational corporations and the sizzling hot media district (complete with Frank Gehry-designed buildings), means that you can pretty much get anything you want – both German items and things missed from back home – in every supermarket in town.

Family life in Düsseldorf is more fragmented than in other parts of Germany. Young people tend to make their own way in life sooner than elsewhere in Germany. This explains the boom in single-apartment dwellings. That's not to say people don't value relationships; rather, parents are as pleased as punch that their children are doing so well.

Most residents of Düsseldorf will judge you not by your politics or purchasing power, but by the choice of district in which you choose to live or centre yourself. Those who like a bit of action will choose Stadtmitte. This multicultural neighbourhood offers both proximity to the financial district and the main shopping drag, the 'Kö' (Königsallee). Slightly more expensive and exclusive is Pempelfort, loved due to its location close to Altstadt.

For the ultimate in cool, you can't beat summer nights in Medienhafen. Order yourself a drink and join the advertising execs as they quaff beer in the sleek and chic bars that line the river.

Finally, don't forget the Japanese. Düsseldorf boasts one of the largest Japanese populations outside Japan. For a night of sushi and karaoke or a day of contemplation in a Japanese garden (without the jetlag a flight to Tokyo entails), look no further.

● *The harbour area represents the ultimate in cool urban living*

Culture

Sophisticates demand the very best, and they certainly don't suffer in Düsseldorf. This city offers some of the finest entertainment around – theatre, opera and orchestral music.

While venues may not be as historically significant as in other locations in the country, you will often find that the acoustics make up for the lack in atmosphere. That, and the quality of the music or dramatics produced.

The most prominent venue in Düsseldorf is the Schauspielhaus (see page 102), a favoured location for fans of high-quality theatre and comedy. Almost all of the performances will be in the German language only, so you will need to know the lingo if you book a ticket. Don't expect anything too adventurous; we're talking strictly middle-of-the-road productions involving well-known German celebrities in 'safe' stagings of both classic and modern works.

For opera and musicals, the Deutsche Oper am Rhein (see page 101) is the place to go. Ballets are also performed at this venue, but the company is less revered. Tickets are well priced, catering for all budgets, ranging from €11–€120.

For classical music, head for the Tonhalle (see page 102). Home to the Düsseldorfer Symphoniker, it is perhaps the most successful modern concert hall in Germany, counting only Berlin's Philharmonie as a rival. Only about a dozen concerts are given each year, and every ticket sells out months in advance. You may want to don black tie or evening gowns if you happen to snag a ticket, as a performance here is considered one of the focal points of the social calendar.

◯ *Enjoy a cultural evening at Deutsche Oper am Rhein*

Another hot ticket is actually outside the city in the nearby town of Wuppertal. Here is the headquarters of legendary choreographer Pina Bausch. She is considered one of the finest contemporary dancers in the world, and the Tanztheater Wuppertal Pina Bausch (see pages 113–15) draws thousands of ardent fans to its stages every year. Bausch has a fervent following among those in the know. If you've never seen (or been interested in) modern dance before, then this is the place to try it. For a sneak preview of what to expect, rent the Pedro Almodovar film *Talk to Her* and see her work in action.

Finally, there is art. While other cities put their money and focus on old masters and traditional paintings, Düsseldorf shuns this trend in favour of the cutting edge, the new and the challenging. The city's best collections all showcase contemporary art and artists. Unlike other museums, the creators who exhibit their works at galleries such as the Kunstsammlung in Ständehaus (see page 84) are very much alive – some straight out of college. You may not like or value everything you see, but the art will definitely make you take a position on its merits – and isn't art made to make you think *and* feel? Locals certainly think so.

● *The WDR television studios in Medienhafen*

Shopping

There is no better city in Germany to shop for high fashion or interior design than in Düsseldorf. This city is known as the place to go to break the bank, due to its reputation as a chic metropolis that has spawned the careers of such big names as Lagerfeld, Jil Sander, JOOP! and Escada.

Düsseldorf's history as an excellent locale for shopping began in 1949 when the nation's first fashion fair and trade exposition brought Christian Dior's 'New Look' to town. Buyers flocked to the city from all over continental Europe, and designers quickly followed suit to try and cash in on the investment potential.

Today, almost all of the big international names have a boutique in Düsseldorf, including Armani, Kenzo and Féraud. Not to mention many other German designers who have stormed the international scene.

The main street in which to stretch your wallet is the Königsallee. Antiques and high-end labels are the focus of this avenue, which is dotted with elegant arcades and everything you could ever want, much of it straight from the catwalk. Even if you aren't considering a purchase, a stroll along the avenue is considered a 'must-do' by locals. Why not stop for a drink in one of the streetside cafés? It is a great tonic after a long day, and provides amazing people-watching and window-shopping opportunities.

Shop opening hours in Düsseldorf are almost the same as you might find in other major European cities, although they are less extensive than in North America. Boutiques will open at

● *Designer Düsseldorf: Königsallee*

around 08.30 or 09.00 and close around 18.30. One night a week will be reserved for late-night shopping – usually a Thursday. Weekend hours vary and you should check ahead to see if the shop you want to visit will definitely be open. Many smaller establishments close at 14.00, although this can vary by season and there are often later openings during the winter months.

For a true bargain, get away from the 'Kö' and head for the flea market at Aachener Platz every Saturday (see map page 80). You may have to do a lot of digging, but real finds can be located if you have the patience.

USEFUL SHOPPING PHRASES

What time do the shops open/close?
Um wieviel Uhr öffnen/schließen die Geschäfte?
Oom veefeel oor erffnen/shleessen dee geshefter?

How much is this?
Wieviel kostet das?
Veefeel kostet das?

Can I try this on?
Kann ich das anprobieren?
Can ikh das anprobeeren?

My size is ...
Ich habe Größe ...
Ikh haber grerser ...

I'll take this one, thank you
Ich nehme das, danke schön
Ikh neymer das, danker shern

This is too large/too small/too expensive
Es ist zu groß/zu klein/zu teuer
Es ist tsu gross/tsu kline/tsu toyer

Eating & drinking

Residents of the Rhine region have a reputation for enjoying life – and food and drink are a natural extension of their *joie de vivre*. The Altstadt has been described numerous times as the 'world's longest bar' due to the volume of drinking establishments that are located in this district. One local speciality that must be tried while exploring the bar scene is Altbier, a dark beer produced in breweries scattered throughout the city. It's quite a heavy brew, but is extremely tasty. Non-drinkers will find it a little more challenging than the more famous Kölsch of Cologne, yet infinitely more satisfying. You'll find Altbier on tap at almost every pub and restaurant in town. No summer weekend is complete without stopping off in one of the beer gardens to chat about what's hot and who's hip.

When entering a bar, it is wise to be aware of drinking etiquette in order to avoid an unintentional slight. As beers are served in smaller glasses in Düsseldorf, groups of friends often purchase rounds. Less quantity served more frequently is how it's done in these parts – and a round is always accompanied by a toast of *Prosit*, which means 'May it be useful'.

Due to the number of expense account travellers who visit the city, and the high standard of living among locals, dining out

PRICE RATING

Price ratings in this book are based on the average price of a main dish without drinks.

£ up to €10   ££ €10–€20   £££ more than €20

in Düsseldorf has a reputation for being expensive – but it doesn't have to be. If you ask a local where they recommend for dinner, they will invariably suggest a 5-star eatery because they want to showcase the culinary delights their city has to offer. Delve a little deeper, however, and each resident is sure to have a special favourite tucked away in their memory banks that doesn't cost a fortune to enjoy.

For sleek and chic eating, join the throngs at Medienhafen, the headquarters of most of the big media and advertising agencies in town. Where there is money, there is fine dining, and this neighbourhood is no exception. In summer, the location on the banks of the Rhine makes eating here a real pleasure.

⬥ Düsseldorf delis are the best in the region

The fact that there is a large international community in the city contributes to the flavours and diversity of restaurants as demands for the tastes of home run high. You'll find fewer German establishments and more 'ethnic' eateries in this city than in almost any other in the nation. Only Berlin could claim to have a more multicultural mélange – and that is primarily due to the massive Turkish population to be found there.

If you're really hankering after German food, you won't be at a loss for places to eat in. Intimate, atmospheric eateries can be found almost everywhere, dishing up the specialities of North Rhine-Westphalia, including *Rheinischer Sauerbraten* (marinated beef) and *Rievkooche* (potato pancakes). Local food tends to be heavy on starches and meats, meaning that vegetarians may have difficulty finding items on a menu. When in doubt, ask the waiter. Other favourites include *Himmel un Äd* (heaven and earth) – a mash of puréed apples and potatoes dished up with fried blood sausage – and *Halve Hahn* (half a chicken), which actually contains no chicken at all; it's actually a roll made from rye filled with cheese. Sausage, while still a popular product here, is less linked with this region than with other parts of the country. Instead, the area is known for its cured hams and meats. Some of the best delicatessens outside of the Black Forest can be found here, providing fantastic flavours for the city's tables.

Desserts are a speciality of the region, often incorporating the fresh produce of the area. Typical sweet dishes will include locally grown cherries and berries, often served with cream or rice pudding.

Entertainment & nightlife

A glass of wine. A spot of jazz. A live concert. A river cruise. Residents of Düsseldorf like the finer things in life when they have a moment of free time. The city of Düsseldorf doesn't really stand out when it comes to after-dark entertainment offerings. It isn't a techno hotspot like Berlin, a sin city like Hamburg, a cultural city like Munich or a gay party Mecca like Cologne. Instead, it takes little bits of all of these cities and offers everything to its residents in one convenient package.

During the week, many locals spend their time in the bars of Medienhafen. Tuesday nights are especially popular, and the sleek and chic watering holes of this modern quarter become flooded with workers in the creative industries as they let off a little midweek steam. Look out for discount drink offers and themed nights.

Weekends are spent in the beerhalls of the Altstadt (Old Town), especially during the Karneval season (see page 14) when tourists and locals alike come together to celebrate the traditions, songs and spirit of the region.

Live music is another popular pastime – usually (but not limited to) sounds with an industrial feel. Kraftwerk remains the most well-known product of Düsseldorf's music scene; however, other bands such as the punk band Die Toten Hosen also have an international following. For big international names, Tor-3 (see page 102) is the usual place to look. Performers such as Radiohead and Robbie Williams have played here at some point during their careers.

Jazz music is another favourite among discerning Düsseldorfers. So much so that there is a venue dedicated solely to its performance. Jazz-Schmiede (see page 89), in the south of the city, brings in both local and international talent. On Tuesday nights, there is an improvised jazz session. You can even get up and join in the fun if you're feeling brave enough yourself.

USEFUL DINING PHRASES

I would like a table for ... people
Ein Tisch für ... Personen, bitte
Ine teesh foor ... perzohnen, bitter

Waiter/waitress!
Herr Ober/Fräulein, bitte!
Hair ohber/froyline, bitter!

May I have the bill, please?
Die Rechnung, bitte?
Dee rekhnung, bitter?

I am a vegetarian. Does this contain meat?
Ich bin Vegetarier (Vegetarierin fem.). Enthält das hier Fleisch?
Ish bin veggetaareer (veggetaareerin). Enthelt dass heer flyshe?

Where is the toilet (restroom) please?
Wo sind die Toiletten, bitte?
Voo zeent dee toletten, bitter?

I would like a cup of/two cups of/another coffee/tea
Eine Tasse/Zwei Tassen/noch eine Tasse Kaffee/Tee, bitte
Ikh merkhter iner tasser/tsvy tassen kafey/tey, bitter

I would like a beer/two beers, please
Ein Bier/Zwei Biere, bitte
Ine beer/tsvy beerer, bitter

● Roncalli's Apollo – follow the bright lights for an evening's fun

Dance clubs are scattered throughout the city, with house and techno ruling the roost in most venues. The most exclusive clubs are situated close to Königsallee; however, there is a growing movement to transform some of the city's abandoned warehouses in the suburbs into industrial discos, thereby emulating those of Cologne and Berlin. Check websites such as www.residentadvisor.net for the latest news in English on clubs and club nights around the city.

An elegant evening can be passed enjoying a sunset cruise. This is certainly a pleasant way to relax, while taking in river views too (see page 84). This option is only available during the warmer months of the year, however, as the Rhine can get decidedly chilly during the winter. When this is not a possibility, go instead to the revolving restaurant at the Rheinturm (see pages 79 and 88) for a meal with a view.

Finally, life isn't always a cabaret, but there are still examples of this traditional German art form in venues around town. The best show can be found at **Roncalli's**, near the Landtag on the banks of the Rhine (see page 89). It may not be to everyone's tastes, but it's certainly worth experiencing if you want a taste of local popular culture.

Sport & relaxation

Despite the fact that there isn't a lot of parkland in Düsseldorf, locals are extremely active. Due to the city's location on the banks of the Rhine, watersports such as sailing and rowing are popular pastimes. For a spot of jogging, many locals choose the trails in the Hofgarten or the pathway that runs along the Rheinufer and for 16 km (10 miles) along the riverside from Medienhafen to the Yacht Club. Alternatively, go further afield

● *The LTU arena is home to Fortuna Düsseldorf*

and head out to the Nordpark in the north of the city or to the lush Grafenberg Forest in the southeast.

There are a number of swimming pools dotted around the city, many with sauna and massage facilities. In summer, outside pools come into their own, offering separate children's entertainment, wave machines and waterslides. A full list of pool locations and facilities can be found at
Ⓦ www.baeder-duesseldorf.de

Private gyms are almost a way of life for Düsseldorf residents, especially for members of the 'image is everything' media crowd. The British chain Holmes Place has two gyms in the city located on Provinzialplatz and the Königsallee. If you are a member of Holmes Place in the UK, it may be possible to use the facilities in Düsseldorf either free of charge or for a reduced cost. The Provinzialplatz gym is especially well regarded due to its stunning pool, which features a glass window on the bottom that looks onto the street below. For a full list of gym locations, go to Ⓦ www.fitnesswelt.de and search under the heading 'Fitness-Studios'.

Golfers are well served by the facilities available in and around the North Rhine region. The closest courses to Düsseldorf are the Golf Park Meerbusch (Ⓦ www.golfpark-meerbusch.de), Düsseldorfer Golf Club (Ⓦ www.duesseldorfer-golf-club.de) and Kosaido International Golf Club (Ⓦ www.kosaido.de).

If you want to watch some football, visit Fortuna Düsseldorf at the LTU arena (ⓐ Europlatz 5 Ⓦ www.ltuarena.de). The venue also stages major concerts.

Accommodation

The fact that Düsseldorf is primarily a business destination is both good and bad news for the short-break traveller. The good news is that most of the hotels are packed out during the week and empty during the weekends, and deals can be found almost year-round. Exceptions to this rule do occur, especially during the peak Karneval season when there are trade shows in town, or in the run-up to Christmas when the markets and suburban shoppers hit the streets. The bad news is that there are few places of accommodation with character to choose from. Hotels in this city fall firmly into the 'low on design, high on amenities' category.

To get the best package, focus on location and shop around on internet sites or through your agent for the lowest price. As long as you time your stay well, you should be able to find a 5-star property for a no-star budget.

HOTELS
Altstadthotel St Georg £ If your idea of a good holiday is partying till dawn, easy access to alcohol and a buzzing vibe,

---

PRICE RATING
Hotels in Germany are graded according to a star system running from 1 star for a cheap guesthouse to 5 stars for a luxurious property with numerous facilities. The following guide prices are based on the cost of a double or twin room for two people per night.

£ = up to €75　　££ = €75–€150　　£££ = more than €150

then this is the hotel for you. Situated smack-bang in the middle of the Old Town, this hotel features a hip cocktail bar right on the ground floor. ⓐ Hunsrücken Strasse 22 ⓣ 602 230 ⓦ www.hotel-st-georg-dusseldorf.de ⓝ Tram: 703, 706, 712, 713, 715

Diana £ Basic rooms with tiny en-suite bathrooms. Don't go expecting frills – just a well-priced room with a bed. Not very inspiring but good for the price. ⓐ Jahn Strasse 31 ⓣ 375 071 ⓝ Tram: 701, 711

Fürstenhof £–££ A good location in the centre of the city on a pleasant square and good-sized rooms make this a nice option. ⓐ Fürstenplatz 3 ⓣ 386 460 ⓦ www.fuerstenhof-dusseldorf.de ⓝ Tram: 701, 707, 708; Bus: 725

● *The elegant Steigenberger Park-Hotel*

Wurms Hotel £–££ Quality budget property furnished in dark woods with bright soft furnishings. If you're travelling alone, there are rooms reserved just for singles without en-suite facilities that are worth looking into. Bathrooms are a little basic, but give you everything you need. Scheuren Strasse 23 375 001 www.hotel-wurms.de Tram: 734, 741, 752; Bus: 835

Ashley's Garden ££ A place with a bit of character. Too bad it's outside the city centre. If you don't mind being away from the city centre, then book yourself into one of the rooms at this restored villa located 5 km (3 miles) north of the Altstadt. Expect very English interiors, heavy on the chintz and cabbage roses. Furnishings are elegant and perfect for a romantic stay. Karl-Kleppe-Strasse 20 516 1710 www.ashleysgarden.de U-Bahn: Reeserplatz

Carathotel ££ Located on the southern fringes of the Altstadt, this great find offers good-size rooms, bright interiors and great access to both the hip happenings of Medienhafen and the historic finds of the Old Town. Benrather Strasse 7a 13050 www.dus.carat-hotel.de Tram: 703, 706, 712, 713, 715

Günnewig Hotel Esplanade £££ Small, intimate, modern, this comfortable hotel ticks all the boxes, offering everything you would expect plus a pool and sauna. Fürstenplatz 17 386 850 www.guennewig.de Tram: 701, 707, 708; Bus: 725

Hotel Orangerie £££ Boutique chic in the heart of the Altstadt. Combine the ambience of the Old Town with modern design by staying at this stylish property. Although you're in the heart of the action, the location just off the main drag means that it never feels overrun, loud or too busy. ⓐ Bäckergasse 1 ❶ 866 800 ⓦ www.hotel-orangerie-mcs.de Ⓝ Bus: 726

Steigenberger Park-Hotel £££ Quiet, luxurious rooms near both the Hofgarten and the beginning of the Königsallee. You may not get the atmosphere of a central Altstadt location, but the elegance, amenities and proximity to great shopping more than make up for it. ⓐ Corneliusplatz 1 ❶ 13810 ⓦ www.steigenberger.de Ⓝ Tram: 78, 79; Bus: 778

FURNISHED APARTMENTS

Schaper Apartment ££ If you're planning a longer stay, a furnished apartment might suit you and your budget more effectively. Furnished apartments come complete with equipped kitchens, meaning you can save money on dining out. For the ultimate splurge, request the rooftop garden suite. The minimum number of nights that can be booked in any of the apartments is three. ⓐ Höhe Strasse 37–41 ❶ 86 22 11 00 ⓦ www.schaper-apartment.com Ⓝ Tram: 704, 709, 719

HOSTELS

DJH Hostel £ Massive hostel sleeping 250-plus, located across the river from the Old Town. Almost all of the rooms feature four-bed dorms, some with a sink. Transport can be a bit of a pain as it is a minimum ten-minute walk from the nearest U-Bahn station. With luggage, it can feel a lot longer. ⓐ Düsseldorfer Strasse 1 ❶ 557 310 Ⓝ U-Bahn: Luegplatz

THE BEST OF DÜSSELDORF

Düsseldorf is a great place both for a short break or as a base for longer explorations of the Rhine region. Whether it's shopping, sightseeing or relaxation you want, you'll find no better location in which to do it all.

TOP 10 ATTRACTIONS

- **The Altstadt** Düsseldorf's historic quarter. If you only have time to visit one place, make this it (see page 60).

- **Kunstsammlung im Ständehaus** Modern art as you have never seen it before (see page 79).

- *Medienhafen* Architecture by Frank Gehry, sleek warehouse boutiques and cafés – this is what modern living should be all about (see page 90).

- **The 'Kö'** No one can leave Düsseldorf without a spot of shopping on the Königsallee (see page 92).

- **Schloss Jägerhof** Rococo splendour, painted bright pink, that hosts the Goethe-Museum (see page 93).

- **Tonhalle** As home to the local symphony orchestra, the Tonhalle is the hottest performance space in town (see page 102).

- **Hofgarten Park** There aren't many green spaces in this city, and so this relaxing park provides a nice place for a break (see page 93).

- **Pina Bausch** Watch work by the the queen of contemporary dance at her base in Wuppertal (see page 113).

- **Rhine cruises** Why not see the city from a different perspective by riding the Rhine on a tour with a difference (see page 84)?

- **Going for sushi** Düsseldorf has one of the largest Japanese populations outside of Japan and provides a great range of Japanese food. (see page 70).

◐ *The city nestles on the banks of the Rhine*

Here's a quick guide to the highlights that a visit to Düsseldorf can offer, depending on how much time you have available.

HALF-DAY: DÜSSELDORF IN A HURRY

Spend your time patrolling the streets of Altstadt. This Old Town district boasts the best the city has to offer, including the historic Marktplatz and Renaissance-period Rathaus (town hall).

1 DAY: TIME TO SEE A LITTLE MORE

Spend the morning rambling through Altstadt before heading out to the top-class museums and galleries that Düsseldorf hosts. Choose from the Museum Kunst Palast (see page 97) with its extensive collection of European art and glass, the incredible modern and expressionist works in the Kunstsammlung Nordrhein-Westfalen: K20 Kunstsammlung am Grabbeplatz (see page 66), or the city's newest art museum, the cutting-edge Kunstsammlung Nordrhein-Westfalen: K21 Kunstsammlung im Ständehaus (see page 79).

2–3 DAYS: SHORT CITY-BREAK

Wander through the Old Town and explore the city museums. Combine this with a night of sipping and supping in Medienhafen, shopping on Königsallee and a mini-Rhine cruise. Be sure to incorporate a trip to Schloss Benrath (see page 105) if you want to add a little history to your Düsseldorf adventure. Or, crash a Karneval party if you happen to be visiting town during the season.

LONGER: ENJOYING DÜSSELDORF TO THE FULL

Get more out of your stay by heading out of town. Travel to the historic city of Cologne (Köln), located just 50 km (31 miles) away (see page 116). Visit the famous cathedral, explore the old town, and purchase a phial of the cologne for which the city is named (or vice versa, depending on which story you hear). Even better, take a boat along the Rhine and cruise your way between Düsseldorf and Cologne (see page 84).

● *Bright and beautiful: the Old Town*

Something for nothing

Düsseldorf for free? Well, that's a challenge. Most sights in this city will cost you. Admission charges aren't usually all that expensive, but if it's free stuff you're after, you may have to be a little creative with your itinerary planning.

The best way to make a euro last is to plan for a lot of walking. A stroll through the Altstadt is one of the best ways to get a flavour of Düsseldorf's look, feel and history. Not only are the cobbled and winding streets highly atmospheric, they're also the best place for a spot of people-watching – one of the best entertainment options in town.

For peace and tranquillity, head to Hofgarten, where you can wander through the sculpture garden commemorating some of the city's most treasured former residents. Alternatively, go to the EKO – The House of Japanese Culture (see page 70) on Brüggener Weg in Niederkassel, where you can learn about Japanese tea ceremonies, register for an Ikebana class, practise your calligraphy or learn more about Japanese current events – for free!

Architecture is one of the prime reasons to come to Düsseldorf, and the district of Medienhafen is the place to go to discover some of Europe's finest modern work. Buildings designed by such luminaries as Frank Gehry can be found in this restored warehouse district, which formerly housed the commercial port of the city. While you won't be able to mix with the in-crowd as they sup and slurp in the chichi eateries and bars of the neighbourhood, you won't feel disappointed: the design of the area is adequately filling for the soul.

A cruise along the Rhine might be nice if you've the cash, but you can also absorb the sights on foot by crossing the river and walking along the shore in Oberkassel. Like many city left banks, this neighbourhood has a bohemian vibe, and the trails that pass along the waterfront have a very rustic feel. The views of the city at sunset are particularly inspiring.

⬥ *The Rheinturm at sunset*

When it rains

Are there a few drops dampening your spirits? Don't let them get to you! Instead, revive your passion for culture and art by heading to one of the major art museums of the city. The collections of the major galleries range from prime examples of old masters and German big names through to the most modern of works still fresh from the artist's studio.

For the classics, it's the Museum Kunst Palast (see page 97) with its extensive holdings of European art from the Middle Ages to the dawn of the 20th century. Of particular note is the glass collection, which is truly wondrous even for those who know little about the art form.

Fast-forward a century and head over to Kunstsammlung Nordrhein-Westfalen: K20 Kunstsammlung am Grabbeplatz (see page 66) if modern art is more to your liking. Impressionists, surrealists and modern Americans all get wall space. Look out for works from the paintbrushes of Henri Matisse, Salvador Dalí, Jackson Pollock and, of course, Paul Klee – the Swiss artist who once lived in Düsseldorf.

Finally, if you prefer to be really challenged by art, then it's the Kunstsammlung Nordrhein-Westfalen: K21 Kunstsammlung im Ständehaus (see page 84) for you. This inspiring gallery only features works produced from 1980 onwards and the results can sometimes be truly challenging.

Not everyone can be an art fan, however, so don't despair if a day staring at paintings and sculpture sends you to sleep. Instead, why not flex your spending power with a trip down to the shopping centres on the Königsallee? This grand avenue, designed in the 19th century, is considered one of the most sophisticated in Europe. The Kö Galerie and Kö Center (see pages 97–8) are the two most popular places in which to spend your hard-earned euros. Here you will find some of the biggest names in fashion and design, including Chanel and Louis Vuitton. The 'ladies who lunch' brigade considers a trip here a daily ritual, making it a fantastic place for a spot of exclusive people-watching.

◆ *Art at the cutting edge: the K20 gallery*

On arrival

TIME DIFFERENCES

German clocks follow Central European Time (CET). During Daylight Saving Time (end Mar–end Oct), the clocks are put ahead one hour. In the German summer, at 12.00, time elsewhere is as follows:

Australia Eastern Standard Time 20.00, Central Standard Time 19.30, Western Standard Time 18.00

New Zealand 22.00

South Africa 12.00

UK and Republic of Ireland 11.00

US and Canada Newfoundland Time 07.30, Atlantic Canada Time 07.00, Eastern Standard Time 06.00, Central Time 05.00, Mountain Time 04.00, Pacific Time 03.00, Alaska 02.00

ARRIVING

By air

Travellers who fly to Düsseldorf will most likely land at one of three airports, depending on which airline is chosen. The most convenient departure and arrival point is **Düsseldorf International Airport** (ⓘ 4210 Ⓦ www.duesseldorf-international.de), located 8 km (5 miles) north of the city centre. As the third largest airport in Germany after Munich and Frankfurt, it is well served by a number of carriers, both low cost and scheduled. Non-stop service is also available from the USA and Ireland. To get to the city centre, take the S-Bahn shuttle 1 or 7 straight to Hauptbahnhof. The journey time is 15 minutes. Alternatively, a taxi will run to about €15.

⬥ Explore the city by bike

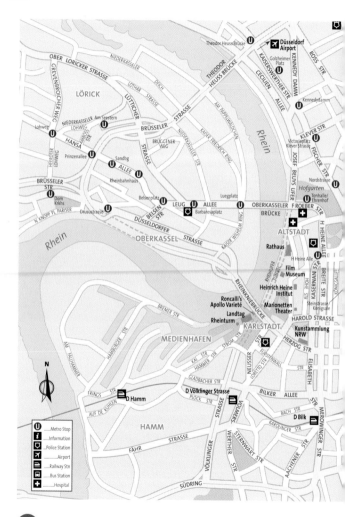

Less convenient is **Köln/Bonn International Airport** (☎ 02203 404 001 🌐 www.airport-cgn.de). Choose this gateway only if you get a really good deal or if you plan on doing a lot of explorations around North Rhine-Westphalia. Buses run to Düsseldorf on a regular basis and take about an hour. A taxi can cost up to €80 one way, depending on traffic.

Finally, if you fly with Ryanair, you will land at **Niederrhein Airport** (☎ 02837 666 000). Located close to the Dutch border, it's a one-hour trip to get into Düsseldorf. The most affordable

● *Heading towards the airport on the A44 bridge*

and convenient method is to take the transfer bus organised by the airline, costing approximately €16.

Airlines
Air Berlin ☎ 0870 738 8880 ⓦ www.airberlin.com
British Airways ☎ 0870 850 9850 ⓦ www.ba.com
Delta ☎ 0845 600 0950 ⓦ www.delta.com
easyJet ☎ 0905 821 0905 ⓦ www.easyjet.com
Lufthansa ☎ 0870 8377 747 ⓦ www.lufthansa.com
Ryanair ⓦ www.ryanair.com

By rail
The main train station servicing Düsseldorf is the **Hauptbahnhof**. Both international and suburban trains arrive

---

IF YOU GET LOST, TRY …

Excuse me, do you speak English?
Entschuldigen Sie, sprechen Sie Englisch?
Entshuldigen zee, shprekhen zee english?

Excuse me, is this the right way to the old town/the city centre/the tourist office/the station/the bus station?
Entschuldigung, geht es hier zur Altstadt/zur Stadtmitte/zur Touristeninformation/zum Bahnhof/zum Busbahnhof?
Entshuldeegoong, gayt es here tsoor altshtat/tsoor shtatmitter/zur touristeninformatsion/tsoom baanhof/tsoom busbaanhof?

Can you point to it on my map?
Können Sie es mir bitte auf der Karte zeigen?
Kernen see es meer bitter owf der kaarte tsygen?

and depart at this main terminus. Due to the city's location in the main industrial sector of the nation, the train links to and from Düsseldorf are extensive. Regular services link the city with Frankfurt, Munich, Berlin and points beyond and in between throughout the day.

By road

Düsseldorf is an extremely easy city to drive in. Streets are wide and well signed. Heavy traffic is usually limited only to the rush hours, but the motorway between the city and Cologne is almost permanently busy with commuters. If you are driving from the UK, you will most likely enter Germany through the Netherlands near Utrecht. From here, it's an easy drive straight along the A3 Autobahn until you reach your destination.

FINDING YOUR FEET

Düsseldorf's city centre is compact and easily walkable. However, the further you go from the Old Town, the greater the distances become. An extensive U-Bahn/S-Bahn network serves the bulk of the city, but you will probably have little need of it as most of the main tourist attractions are centrally located.

ORIENTATION

The bombing of Düsseldorf gave city planners the opportunity to start afresh after World War II. The fact that they decided to retain the original street plan has done wonders for the character of the historic Altstadt but may challenge you when it comes to navigation.

The main tourist quadrant of the Old Town lies on the banks of the Rhine and is bordered to the north by the Hofgarten, to the east by Heinrich Heine Allee and to the south by Harold Strasse. This is likely to be where you will spend the bulk of your time.

Further south along the Rhine banks, about 200 m (218 yds) from Harold Strasse, is the ultra-modern Medienhafen. Come here for top-notch mixing and mingling with the city's in-crowd and media moguls.

South of Harold Strasse lies the redeveloped commercial and residential district of Karlstadt; while the Japanese Quarter around Immermann Strasse and Königsallee are to the east of Heinrich Heine Allee.

GETTING AROUND
Public transport
Düsseldorf can be navigated by U-Bahn trains, trams and buses. Transport is extremely efficient and runs like clockwork. Thank goodness for German precision. The city is divided into zones, with journeys priced according to how many zones you cross during your trip. Single tickets cost approximately €2 for one zone, €3 for two zones and €7 for three zones. If you think you will be using the system often, invest in a carnet of four tickets at a cost of around €6 for a single zone, €11 for two zones and €24 for all three zones. The likelihood of you needing two- or three-zone tickets is little – unless you plan explorations into the surrounding countryside or suburbs.

Day passes cost approximately €7 (1 zone), €10 (1–2 zones) or €18 (1–3 zones), and can be used by up to five people at a time.

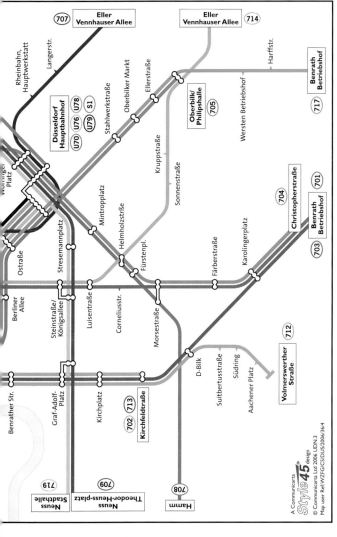

Purchase tickets from bus drivers or by using the orange vending machines at bus, tram and U-Bahn stops. Remember: you must validate your ticket when you board or you will be subject to a fine.

Alternatively take to two wheels. Many hostels and hotels will hire out bicycles for sightseeing.

CAR HIRE

Unless you are planning drives out to explore the countryside or points further afield, you won't need to hire a car. In the event that you do decide to get some wheels, you should have few problems as the German Autobahn and street system around Düsseldorf is efficient and well maintained. Like in any other city, road rage is always something to look out for, but the wide multi-laned Autobahns and good paving mean that altercations are few and far between.

As Düsseldorf is a destination primarily for the business traveller, rental rates can be quite high. There are always more premium and luxury cars to choose from at an agency as they cater for travellers with expense accounts. The minimum age for renting an economy car is 21.

Europcar ⓐ Konrad-Adenauer-Platz 11 ⓣ 173 810 ⓦ www.europcar.com

Hertz ⓐ Immermann Strasse 65 ⓣ 357 025 ⓦ www.hertz.com

ⓞ *Bird's-eye view from the Rheinturm*

Altstadt

The Old Town (Altstadt) of Düsseldorf is the place to go if you want to see the roots of one of Germany's most intriguing cities. It was within these winding streets that the Electors built an industrial powerhouse that ruled the economic waves of the Rhine.

While much of the neighbourhood was destroyed by Allied bombing in World War II, most of the buildings have been restored to their original splendour. The best museums, finest examples of old architecture and most atmospheric eateries can all be found within the lanes of Altstadt. If you have but a few hours in town, then this is the place to go to soak in all the German atmosphere.

SIGHTS & ATTRACTIONS

Mahnund Gedenkstätte für die Opfer des Nationalsozialismus

This memorial examines National Socialism and the victims of the Holocaust. Exhibits look at the role the city played in the extermination of Jews, homosexuals, gypsies and political opponents, in addition to examining the resistance movement that worked against Hitler's policies. Today, Düsseldorf has the third largest population of Jews in the country, with many of the survivors of the 'Final Solution' having returned to their homes following the end of the war.

ⓐ Mühlen Strasse 29 ⓣ 899 6205 ⓛ 11.00–17.00 Tues–Fri & Sun, 13.00–17.00 Sat ⓝ U-Bahn: Heinrich-Heine-Allee

⬥ *Enchanting architecture in Altstadt*

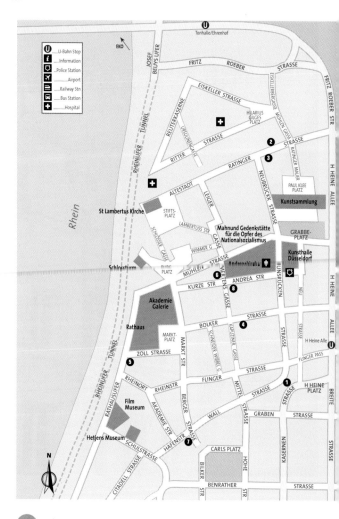

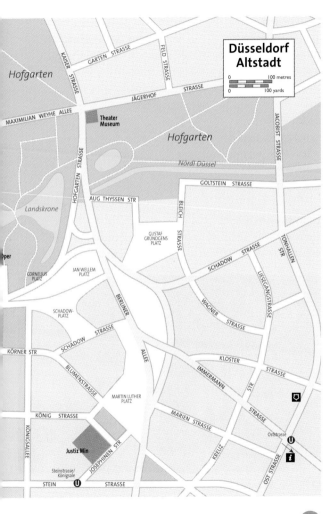

Düsseldorf Altstadt

0   100 metres
0   100 yards

Hofgarten

KAISER STRASSE

GARTEN STRASSE

FELD STRASSE

STRASSE

JÄGERHOF

MAXIMILIAN WEYHE ALLEE

JACOBIST STRASSE

Theater Museum

HOFGARTEN STRASSE

Hofgarten

Nördl Düssel

GOLTSTEIN STRASSE

AUG THYSSEN STR

BLEICH STRASSE

Landskrone

GUSTAF GRÜNDGENS PLATZ

TONHALLEN STR

SCHADOW STRASSE

LIESEGANGSTRASSE

per

CORNELIUS PLATZ

JAN WELLEM PLATZ

BERLINER

WAGNER STRASSE

SCHADOW-PLATZ

ALLEE

SCHADOW STRASSE

KÖRNER STR

KLOSTER STRASSE

BLUMENSTRASSE

IMMERMANN STR

KÖNIG STRASSE

MARTIN LUTHER PLATZ

MARIEN STRASSE

KÖNIGSALLEE

Oststrasse U

Justiz Min

JOSEPHINEN STR

KREUZ

OST STRASSE

Steinstrasse/ Königsalle

STEIN U STRASSE

Schlossturm

The powerful de Berg family founded the city, and this 13th-century tower is all that remains from the structure of the original castle that fortified the settlement. The building now calls itself home to the Schiffahrtsmuseum, which is dedicated to chronicling over two millennia of boatbuilding and activity on the Rhine river.

ⓐ Burgplatz 30 ⓣ 899 4195 ⓛ 11.00–18.00 ⓝ U-Bahn: Heinrich Heine Allee. Admission charge

CULTURE

Film Museum

Germany's film industry traces its early roots back to Düsseldorf, which once housed the bulk of production and direction for the

ⓐ *The Film Museum chronicles the history of German cinema*

nation. This museum takes a look at the early days of German film and chronicles how it has developed over the decades; it is certainly worth a look for ardent film fanatics. A Black Box cinema offers regular screenings of obscure finds and art-house classics. Check listings for details.

ⓐ Schulstrasse 4 ⓣ 899 2232 ⓛ 11.00–17.00 Tues & Thur–Sun, 11.00–21.00 Wed ⓝ Bus: 726. Admission charge

Hetjens Museum

This is the only museum in the country dedicated solely to the art of ceramics. Over 8,000 works are on display, including items from Asia, Europe and beyond. It's interesting to realise the impact that ceramics had on the economies of years gone by, especially following the introduction of trade routes from Asia during the Middle Ages. You can see why merchants were inspired when you walk through this fascinating collection.

ⓐ Schulstrasse 4 ⓣ 899 4210 ⓛ 11.00–17.00 Tues & Thur–Sun, 11.00–21.00 Wed ⓝ Bus: 726. Admission charge

Kunsthalle Düsseldorf

The city's second-most 'out there' modern art museum is a showcase for the new, the disturbing, the provocative and the downright questionable. Temporary exhibits provide the draw. Be sure to check listings in advance to see if what's on display will appeal to you and/or be suitable for children.

ⓐ Grabbeplatz 4 ⓣ 899 6240 ⓛ 12.00–19.00 Tues–Thur & Sat, 12.00–21.00 Fri, 11.00–18.00 Sun ⓝ U-Bahn: Heinrich-Heine-Allee. Admission charge

Kunstsammlung Nordrhein-Westfalen: K20 Kunstsammlung am Grabbeplatz

There are two museums in one at this slick modern building featuring the best in modern art. The better museum of the two is arguably the K20, but both are of interest and well worth

⬤ *Experience a day on the tiles at the Hetjens Museum*

spending a few hours exploring. The most notable highlights of the collection include a vast selection of works by Paul Klee, a Swiss painter who once resided in the city while he taught at the National Academy of Art. Surrealist art is another focal point for the collection, including works by the king of the movement, Salvador Dalí. Other big names worth checking out include Pablo Picasso, Jackson Pollock and Henri Matisse. Be sure to stop by the permanent exhibit of American works dating from 1946. Temporary exhibits often descend on the building, with six big collections brought in throughout the year for two-month spells. Check the schedule in advance to see if there is a large-scale show worth tying into your visit.

ⓐ Grabbeplatz 5 ❶ 838 1130 ⓦ www.kunstsammlung.de ⓛ 10.00–18.00 Tues–Fri, 11.00–18.00 Sat & Sun, 10.00–22.00 1st Wed of every month Ⓝ U-Bahn: Heinrich Heine Allee. Admission charge

RETAIL THERAPY

Carsch Haus Düsseldorf's favourite department store. Good place to go for clothing basics. ⓐ Heinrich Heine Platz ❶ 83970 ⓦ www.galeria-kaufhof.de ⓛ 09.30–20.00 Mon–Sat Ⓝ U-Bahn: Heinrich Heine Allee

TAKING A BREAK

Pia Eis £ ❶ Forget Italian *gelato* – this ice-cream parlour really knows its stuff. ⓐ Kasernen Strasse 1 ❶ 326 233 ⓛ Vary according to season Ⓝ U-Bahn: Heinrich Heine Allee

JAPANESE QUARTER

So why is Düsseldorf considered something of a little Tokyo? Well, the biggest reason is that it has the third largest population of Japanese on the European continent. For a night of sushi, sake and karaoke, you can't go wrong – especially not in and around the streets of Immermannstrasse where the bulk of the community is located.

Düsseldorf's large Japanese population is due to the number of Japanese multinational companies that base their European operations in and around the city. Where there are Japanese companies, there is a need for Japanese management – and this is the city where they work, live and play. This German–Japanese relationship has been in existence since the 1960s, when both nations were actively rebuilding following the destructive years of World War II. In order to help each other out and to take advantage of the tax breaks offered to companies through the Marshall Plan, Japanese industry moved its European factories to the German city that offered the best infrastructure, had the closest links to the sea, and was on an Autobahn route that linked to the lucrative French markets. Düsseldorf was the natural choice.

The city actively supports its foreign-born residents and celebrates their culture regularly in the form of the annual Japan Day celebrations held in Altstadt every May. Beginning in the early afternoon, live Japanese entertainment is showcased from a stage on Burgplatz, and the Rhine embankment is transformed into a Japanese-themed funfair which ends in a spectacular display of Japanese pyrotechnics once the sun sets. The large stage on Burgplatz is the scene of Japanese dance, song and theatre shows, while the Rhine embankment is

◆ *A little piece of Japan in Germany at EKO*

taken over by the Japanese government as it sponsors various artistic organisations through a cultural exchange programme to display Samurai feats, Ikebana floral demonstrations, calligraphy or Origami, and Japanese sports such as Kendo and Judo. You can learn how to put on a kimono or take an instant Japanese–German mini-language course. A joint *bon-dance* (Japanese folk dance) by the Rhine rounds off the event.

To fully experience the Japanese community at its finest, head for Immermannstrasse and the streets in and around the Hotel Nikko. Here you will find Japanese food shops, sushi bars, karaoke parlours and *manga* comic-sellers. You'll also spot a branch of the famous Mitsukoshi department store. Alternatively, head over to Niederkassel and walk to Brüggener Weg 6, home to **EKO – The House of Japanese Culture**, an intriguing centre with a goal to introduce Japanese culture to the community and to act as a central point for Japanese residents to congregate socially. Pop inside to enjoy a spot of tea in the tearoom, meditate in the Japanese gardens or worship at the temple, the only one of its kind outside of Japan.

For food, there are practically dozens of places to choose from. One of the most recommended is, however, away from the main action on Immermannstrasse. Considered the finest in the city, **Daitokai** (Mutter-Ely-Strasse 1, just off Grabbeplatz in the Altstadt) offers a varied menu of favourites that would even impress visitors from Japan.

AFTER DARK

Restaurants

Im Füchschen £ ❷ Typical German beerhall fare and atmosphere. Dishes are heavy on meat and potato combinations. Wash it all down with mugs of the local beer for a filling meal. ⓐ Ratinger Strasse 28 ❶ 137 470 ⓦ www.fuechschen.de ⓛ 09.00–24.00 Mon–Thur, 09.00–01.00 Sat & Sun ⓝ U-Bahn: Tonhalle/Ehrenhof

Ohme Jupp £ ❸ Lightly bohemian café offering breakfasts, bagels and Mediterranean-inspired main courses. ⓐ Ratinger Strasse 19 ❶ 326 406 ⓛ 08.30–01.00 Mon–Sat, 10.00–01.00 Sun ⓝ U-Bahn: Tonhalle/Ehrenhof

Zum Schlüssel £–££ ❹ Authentic brew-pub that produces its own-label beers on the premises. Combine the drink with delicious and hearty German menu items including sausages, sauerkraut, soups, salads and schnitzel. ⓐ Bolker Strasse 43–47 ❶ 828 9550 ⓛ 10.00–24.00 Sun–Thur, 10.00–01.00 Fri & Sat ⓝ U-Bahn: Heinrich Heine Allee

En de Canon ££ ❺ Local favourites compose the menu of this much-loved establishment housed in the city's first post office. The summer beer garden is especially popular. ⓐ Zollstrasse 7 ❶ 329 798 ⓛ 11.30–24.00 ⓝ U-Bahn: Heinrich Heine Allee

Tante Anna ££ ❻ This one is for both meat-lovers and vegetarians. Housed in a restored 16th-century chapel, this delicious restaurant offers some of the best takes on local favourites available. Choose from either the à la carte or affordable set menu. ⓐ Andreasstrasse 2 ⓣ 131 163 ⓦ www.tanteanna.de ⓛ 18.00–23.30 Mon–Sat ⓝ U-Bahn: Heinrich Heine Allee

Zum Schiffchen ££ ❼ You might want to skip a meal or two before coming to this establishment, the oldest in Düsseldorf. In existence since 1628, it names both Heinrich Heine and Napoleon as former diners. Portions are absolutely huge. ⓐ Hafenstrasse 5 ⓣ 132 421 ⓦ www.brauerei-zum-schiffchen.de ⓛ 11.30–24.00 Mon–Sat ⓝ U-Bahn: Heinrich Heine Allee

Zum Csikos ££–£££ ❽ For a truly romantic evening – or if you just want something other than German food – then this Hungarian restaurant will do the trick. Bathed in candlelight, the eatery is housed in a 17th-century townhouse and dishes up yummy goulashes to its dedicated following. ⓐ Andreasstrasse 9 ⓣ 329 771 ⓛ 18.00–03.00 Mon–Sat, 11.00–03.00 Sun ⓝ U-Bahn: Heinrich Heine Allee

Bars, clubs & discos
Brauerei Zum Uel This German tavern is the most popular student spot in town. Prices are cheap for both the filling fare and the beer. If you're looking for information on cultural or political events, then check out the flyers and posters that line the walls. ⓐ Ratinger Strasse 16 ⓣ 325 369 ⓛ 10.00–01.00 Mon–Fri, 12.00–03.00 Sat & Sun ⓝ U-Bahn: Heinrich Heine Allee

Engelchen Live *la vie bohème* at this alternative drinking spot that brings out a who's who of the city's arts-loving crowd. By day, it's a coffee spot; by night, the offerings become more alcoholic. ⓐ Kurze Strasse 15 ⓣ 327 356 ⓛ 11.00–02.00 Mon–Fri, 15.00–05.00 Sat & Sun ⓝ U-Bahn: Heinrich Heine Allee

Kabüffke An old-style pub with a great mix of drinks, including a locally produced herbal schnapps called *Killeptisch*, not available in many other locations. The bar itself is also an attraction, made from hundreds of glass bottles. ⓐ Flinger Strasse 1 ⓣ 133 269 ⓛ 11.00–late ⓝ U-Bahn: Heinrich Heine Allee

McLaughlin's Irish Pub Every city in the world seems to have an Irish pub, and Düsseldorf is no exception. Irish bands and pints of Guinness will make you feel like you're home. ⓐ Kurze Strasse 11 ⓣ 324 611 ⓛ 17.00–01.00 Sun–Thur, 11.00–03.00 Fri & Sat ⓝ U-Bahn: Heinrich Heine Allee

Schnabelewopski Once the home of the writer Heinrich Heine, this intimate pub with a literary bent is named after the character found in Heine's *Memoirs of Herr von Schnabelewopski*. ⓐ Bolker Strasse 53 ⓣ 133 200 ⓛ 12.00–01.00 ⓝ U-Bahn: Heinrich Heine Allee

A WALK THROUGH ALTSTADT

Düsseldorf's oldest quarter is a tourist-friendly district composed of car-free cobblestone lanes, authentic beerhalls and numerous historical sights. Centred on Marktplatz with its restored Renaissance Rathaus (town hall), it's a charming neighbourhood in which to kill a few hours – or a few days.

As much of Düsseldorf was destroyed during World War II, many of the buildings in this quarter are actually recreations of the original structures. Only a handful of buildings are authentic, but it is almost impossible to tell the difference as the rebuilding process was incredibly accurate.

Begin any trip through the Altstadt on the Marktplatz in order to admire both the **Rathaus** and the **statue of the Elector** Jan Wellem on horseback situated directly in front of the building. The Elector was one of the city's most admired leaders, primarily due to his love of the arts and influence on the design of the city. His grave is a short walk away to the north, inside the baroque **Andreaskirche** on Grabbeplatz. The church is one of the best attended in town. The interiors, decorated in white and gold, feature 22 statues of biblical figures. Every day at noon, an organ recital is performed as part of the church's daily services.

From here, it's a few steps west to the **Mahnund Gedenkstätte für die Opfer des Nationalsozialismus** (Memorial for the Victims of the Nazi Regime) (see page 60). This exhibit takes a look at the effect that the

The statue of Jan Wellem dominates Marktplatz

Holocaust had on the city and the efforts made by citizens to combat the National Socialist party. Information in English is available.

Just around the corner from the memorial on Stiftsplatz is the 14th-century **St Lambertus Kirche**. Over the years, the structure has been renovated on a number of occasions, incorporating new styles each and every time expansions were completed. Today, it includes elements of Gothic, Renaissance and baroque architecture, all set off by the extremely lush interiors. Take a look at the spire and note the distortion caused by the unseasoned wood that was used during its construction. The church is now considered a basilica minor (small cathedral) after the Vatican elevated the title of the building in 1974 to honour its role in Christian history.

Further along on Burgplatz lies the **Schlossturm**, the last remaining part of the former Electors' Palace. It now houses a maritime museum dedicated to telling the history of the Rhine and the people who used it for economic and militaristic advantage. Head towards the river in order to finish your tour of the Altstadt at the beginning of the **Rheinuferpromenade**, a spectacular and much-loved walkway that runs along the Rhine above the road tunnel (Rheinufer Tunnel) and stretches as far away as the Rheinpark and Medienhafen.

Karlstadt & City South

The district of Karlstadt was the first 'suburb' of the original Altstadt as residents demanded larger homes, space and light away from the warren-like streets of the Old Town. Development kicked off in the late 18th century, and many of today's buildings reflect the baroque tastes of the day. Today, Karlstadt is the address of choice due to the close proximity it enjoys to the atmospheric Old Town.

Further south and east takes visitors into the more modern neighbourhoods of Medienhafen and City South. This is where you can find the architectural looks of tomorrow, complete with buildings created by some of the leading lights of modern design, including Frank Gehry and David Chipperfield. For more information on this exciting dockside development, see pages 90–1.

SIGHTS & ATTRACTIONS

Architecture

Following World War II, much of Karlstadt was in ruins. The neighbourhood's proximity to the Rhine and its large industrial base made it a prime target for Allied bombers. City planners decided to start from scratch and committed themselves to making the area a showcase for modern architecture. A walk through the district exposes visitors to some of the most striking examples of modern design in Europe, especially near the transformed docks of Medienhafen. One of the best examples is the **Landtag**. Completed in 1988, the Landtag is the home of the state parliament for North Rhine-Westphalia. It's an impressive building – made even more so by its position on the banks of the Rhine, surrounded by parkland. You'll find it immediately next to the Rheinturm, just off Moselstrasse.

Heinrich Heine Institut

Düsseldorf's most famous contribution to the world of literature was Heinrich Heine – a writer who specialised in lyric

◉ *The dramatically lit Rheinturm is a major landmark*

poetry during the early years of the 19th century (see feature pages 82–3). The Institute contains a library, archive and interesting museum.

ⓐ Bilker Strasse 12–14 ☏ 899 571 🕐 09.00–17.00 Mon–Fri, 12.00–16.00 Sun Ⓝ Tram: 704, 707

Rheinturm

Enjoy a spectacular view of the city from this radio tower built between 1979 and 1982 on the banks of the Rhine. Approximately 240 m (787 ft) in height, it functions as directional radio, television and FM transmitter for the region. An intriguing feature of the tower is a special light sculpture that runs along the shaft, which functions as a digital clock. Called the *Lichtzeitpegel* (light time level) it is actually the largest decimal clock in the world. For visitors, a high-speed lift goes up to near the top of the tower. On clear days, you can see as far as Cologne – and beyond. A rooftop revolving restaurant offers a nice set menu for those who want to combine tourism with tasty treats (see page 88 for further details).

ⓐ Strom Strasse 20 ☏ 848 558 🕐 11.00–23.30 Mon–Fri, 10.00–23.30 Sat & Sun Ⓝ Tram: 704, 709, 719; Bus: 725. Admission charge

CULTURE

Kunstsammlung Nordrhein-Westfalen: K21 Kunstsammlung im Ständehaus

Where the famous K20 stops (see page 66), K21 begins. Artwork from 1980 onwards is the focal point of this cutting-edge

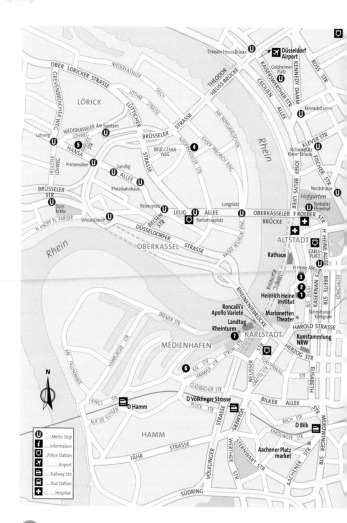

Theodor Heuss Brücke

Düsseldorf
Airport

Golzheimer
Platz

Kennedydamm

Victoriaplatz/
Klever Strasse

Nordstrasse

Tonhalle/
Ehrenhof

OBERKASSELER

BRÜCKE

ALTSTADT

CARLS
PLATZ

Rathaus

Heinrich Heine
Institut

Roncalli's
Apollo Varieté

Landtag
Rheinturm

Marionetten
Theater

KARLSTADT

Kunstsammlung
NRW

MEDIENHAFEN

D Hamm

D Völklinger Strasse

D Bilk

HAMM

Aachener Platz
market

LÖRICK

HANSA

N

Ⓤ	Metro Stop
ℹ	Information
🚓	Police Station
✈	Airport
🚆	Railway Stn
🚌	Bus Station
✚	Hospital

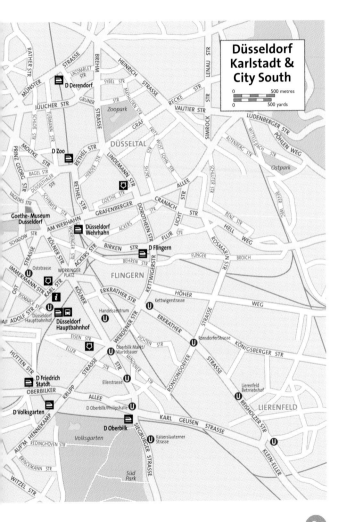

Düsseldorf Karlstadt & City South

0   500 metres
0   500 yards

HEINRICH HEINE

Poet and writer Christian Johann Heinrich Heine is one of Düsseldorf's favourite sons and is considered to be one of the leading lights of 19th-century German literature. Born Chaim Heine to a prominent Jewish family, Heine spent his early years learning the banking trade and studying law, before turning to the field of lyric poetry, a branch of literature that set poems to music by *Lieder* composers. Some of the composers with whom Heine collaborated during his career included Johannes Brahms, Felix Mendelssohn, Franz Schubert, Robert Schumann and Richard Wagner. Love was the emotion that spurred Heine to write most of his famous works, beginning with his *Gedichte* (*Poems*) in 1821.

As Heine grew older, his politics began to influence his work, causing him to leave Germany for France in 1831. While there he fell in with a group of socialists who dreamt of a classless society. This political belief resulted in Heine's permanent exile from Germany as the authorities in his home country banned his works, fearing he might be a bad influence on society.

Heine's works primarily fall into one of two categories: sweeping romance or bitter political satire – usually with German society as his target of choice. Despite the disapproval of many governments, his work continued to be published – usually with the assistance of some of his more famous friends, including Karl Marx.

Heine never lost his love for his homeland, often writing poems that celebrated the nation's beauty.

The poet's ardent nationalism ensured his popularity in Germany until the days of National Socialism, when his Jewish background placed him on a blacklist. The power of his words, however, continued to inspire Nazis; his volumes were attributed to an anonymous writer in order to get around the national anti-Jewish policies.

Heine once stated that, 'Where they burn books, they will, in the end, burn humans too'. These words are now engraved on the ground where the Nazis hosted massive book-burning sessions at Opernplatz in Berlin during 1933.

● *The Heinrich Heine Institut celebrates the writer's life*

museum. The gallery exists to showcase the work of the new millennium – and is often challenging as a result. Conceptual art is a strong point for the museum, along with photography,

CRUISING THE RHINE

No trip to North Rhine-Westphalia is complete without at least an hour or two spent cruising along the river that gave the region its power and prestige – the Rhine. Whether as part of a longer, more extensive cruise itinerary or simply by rented rowboat, a trip on the water gives a whole new perspective to any traveller and caps off the perfect German holiday.

Rhine cruises leave from the docks near Medienhafen and can take you up and down the immediate shore or as far away as Cologne or Mainz, depending on the season and how much time you have available.

Competition for your tourist euro is fierce, so be sure to look out for regular specials such as two-for-one days or senior discounts, especially on the shorter or day-trip itineraries. Wednesdays are often family day, making this a great option if you're travelling with the kids.

One of the best evening options is to take a dinner cruise, which combines your evening meal with a spot of sightseeing. The meal may not be the best you'll experience in the city, but it will certainly be the most visually interesting. Most cruise companies operate between July and September; however, a few shorter-haul operators stretch the season from April to November.

video and film installations. Until the museum becomes full, other galleries and private collectors are constantly donating temporary exhibits to supplement the permanent collection.

ⓐ Ständehausstrasse 1 ⓣ 838 1600 ⓦ www.kunstsammlung.de
ⓛ 10.00–18.00 Tues–Fri, 11.00–18.00 Sat & Sun, 10.00–22.00 1st Wed of every month ⓝ Tram: 703, 706, 712, 713, 715. Admission charge

RETAIL THERAPY

Since the later years of the 18th century when the peaceful neighbourhood of Karlstadt began to develop, a fruit and vegetable market has been held on Carlsplatz to service the needs of residents. Despite the fact that the square is located at the very northern tip of the district, Carlsplatz is considered the heart of the Karlstadt Quarter – and everyone seems to know everyone else in the market as a result.

Antique shops, galleries and dealers also adore Karlstadt, with the best of the bunch setting up shop in the elegant Bilker Strasse, which runs south from Carlsplatz. The further south you go, the more suburban the selection becomes. As soon as you pass Graf-Adolf-Strasse, the sophistication of the Königsallee is left behind to be replaced by the southern city 'shopping mile' – a collection of shops geared towards the needs of residents rather than tourists.

Arts Decoratifs For art deco works, Germany is always the best place to head. This boutique offers the finest examples in the city. Portable items include jewellery and interiors such as lamps and vases. Hohestrasse 20 324 553 11.00–18.00 Mon–Sat U-Bahn: Heinrich Heine Allee

Lothar Heubel Go with a full wallet if you want to pick up any of the Asian or African treasures on display at this find of an antique boutique. Everything is of the finest quality. Bastion Strasse 27 134 103 www.heubel.de 09.30–18.00 Mon–Sat U-Bahn: Heinrich Heine Allee

TAKING A BREAK

Bim's Marktwirtschaft £ ❶ This perfect breakfast place is also good for snacks and late-night drinks. Cosy up in one of the leather banquettes and down either a filling early meal or soothe your feet after a day of shopping. Benrather Strasse 7 327 185 08.00–01.00 U-Bahn: Heinrich Heine Allee

Herr Spoerl Deli £ ❷ Düsseldorf's young, hip and trendy crowd love this place – drawn by the fresh quiches, soups and deli sandwiches (and excellent people-watching). Go hungry and you won't be disappointed. Benrather Strasse 6a 323 8211 10.00–22.00 U-Bahn: Heinrich Heine Allee

AFTER DARK

Restaurants
Fischhaus £–££ ❸ As it sounds, this restaurant offers a great menu of freshly caught fish dishes. Menus change according to

the season. ❸ Berger Strasse 3–7 ❶ 854 9864 ⓦ www.fischhaus-duesseldorf.de ⏰ 11.30–24.00 Ⓝ U-Bahn: Heinrich Heine Allee

Im Alten Bierhaus £–££ ❹ Across the river from the Altstadt, this high-class wine bar/tavern dates its existence back to the year 1641. Food is typically German in flavour. Sundays bring dedicated beer drinkers in order to quaff mugs of the local Altbier. ❸ Niederkasseler Strasse 75 ❶ 551 272 ⏰ 15.00–24.00 Tues–Sat, 11.00–23.00 Sun Ⓝ Bus: 834

De' Medici ££ ❺ Fine Italian fare that moves away from standard pastas and tomato bases. Go for lightly grilled fish and succulent meats. The side dishes are always great, so be sure to order a few to go with your main course. ❸ Amboss-Strasse 3 ❶ 594 151 ⏰ 12.00–14.30, 18.00–22.00 Sun–Fri, 18.00–22.00 Sat Ⓝ U-Bahn: Prinzenallee

▲ Tickle your tastebuds with traditional pork knuckle

Berens am Kai £££ Mix and mingle with the media types at this exclusive eatery in the heart of Medienhafen. By day, this is the favoured business lunch spot for the various internet entrepreneurs, documentary filmmakers, ad execs and newspaper publishers who work in the neighbourhood. From the outside, the office-block architecture may not inspire. The food and service, however, more than make up for this lack of artistic architecture. By night, the views of the harbour are stunning and the place becomes a romantic date spot. The modern twist on German dishes may make you rethink your thoughts on national cuisine – in a good way. ⓐ Kaistrasse 16 ⓣ 300 6750 ⓛ 12.00–15.00, 18.30–24.00 Mon–Fri, 18.30–24.00 Sat ⓝ S-Bahn: Völklinger Strasse

Rheinturm Top 100 Restaurant £££ ⓞ You have to love revolving restaurants – they may be tourist traps, but you can't beat the views – and this dining spot delivers both panoramas and yummy nibbles. Everything is seasonal, drawing from the best produce of the region. Thankfully for vegetarians, there are plenty of options. ⓐ Strom Strasse 20 ⓣ 848 558 ⓛ 12.00–14.30, 15.00–17.00, 18.30–23.00 ⓝ Tram: 704, 709, 719; Bus: 725

Bars, clubs & discos

MK-2 This buzzing nightclub is situated in the heart of Medienhafen and is best known for its popular after-work Tuesday house nights. Also packed on weekends, it draws a mix of suits and chics depending on who is spinning behind the decks. ⓐ Kai Strasse 4 ⓣ 303 3905 ⓦ www.mk-2.de ⓛ 20.00–late Tues–Sat ⓝ S-Bahn: Völklinger Strasse

Zum Uerige For the typical Oktoberfest experience all year-round, go to this very 'olde-German' style tavern where the floor is covered in puddles of beer from the copious mugs poured out by the waiters every second. During Karneval time, this is the place to be. ⓐ Berger Strasse 1 ⓣ 11.00–24.00 Ⓝ U-Bahn: Heinrich Heine Allee

Cinemas & theatres

Jazz-Schmiede Fantastic jazz venue featuring both international big names and local bands. Tuesday nights offer free jam sessions which are well worth the jaunt away from the city centre. ⓐ Himmelgeisterstrasse 107 ⓣ 311 0564 Ⓦ www.jazz-schmiede.de ⓛ Vary according to performance schedule Ⓝ Tram: 706

Marionetten-Theater You might think that a puppet theatre is strictly for children – but you'd be wrong. This amazing marionette troupe puts on incredible displays of virtuoso puppetry featuring full-scale operas and plays. ⓐ Bilker Strasse 7 ⓣ 328 432 Ⓦ www.marionettentheater-duesseldorf.de ⓛ 13.00–18.00 Tues–Sat Ⓝ U-Bahn: Heinrich Heine Allee

Roncalli's Apollo Varieté Popular variety and cabaret theatre featuring juggling, acrobats and comedians. Almost like a German version of a Las Vegas floor show. ⓐ Haroldstrasse 1 ⓣ 828 9090 Ⓦ www.apollo-variete.com ⓛ Hours vary according to performance schedule Ⓝ U-Bahn: Poststrasse

MEDIENHAFEN

For years, the port of Düsseldorf was a blight on the river landscape, scarring the city with its uninspiring architecture, abandoned factories and empty storage spaces.

When the state parliament decided to build its new headquarters here, many people were sceptical, but money began to flood in, and developers saw the potential of the area for restoration, recreation and modernisation.

Internationally renowned architects were called in to create a 'media community' of residences, office buildings, shops and centres that would energise the city and create a focal point for the creative industries.

Frank Gehry was just one of the acclaimed architects to stamp their style on the neighbourhood. Others who have contributed to the region include David Chipperfield, Steven Holl, Joe Coenen, Claude Vasconi and Fuminiko Maki. The result is an eclectic mix of postmodern design that works due to its higgledy-piggledy, yet organic layout.

Fewer than 2,000 inhabitants currently live in Medienhafen, but that figure is rising every day as builders introduce more and more condominiums and apartments to the area. Popular with singles, it's a buzzing neighbourhood that offers clubs, cocktail bars and restaurants. These really come into their own during the summer months, taking advantage of the riverside location.

Architectural tours of Medienhafen featuring lectures and talks from specially trained guides can be arranged. Book your tour through ⓦ www.medienhafen.de

⬤ *Modern architecture never looked so good: Medienhafen*

Königsallee & Hofgarten

At the beginning of the 19th century, the Altstadt was starting to get a little crowded. The Industrial Revolution was just around the corner, Rhine river traffic was bringing trade and finance to the city, and the city needed to spread outside its confines. The natural choice was to go east away from the river – and a new neighbourhood was born.

The first street to be created was the elegant Königsallee, a broad avenue intended to become the main street in the community. The Electors wanted to spark a desire to transform the city into a calm oasis of ponds, greenery and canals, and they largely succeeded thanks to the popularity of this new, grand thoroughfare. The bulk of the city elite transplanted themselves to the area, turning the 'Kö' into the address of choice for those with the financial resources to afford it.

Today, Königsallee is one of the most famous streets in Germany – however, it is far from the nation's most beautiful. Wartime bombing destroyed much of the architecture of the west side of the street. Office buildings, banks and airline ticketing branches are now in this section. Instead, stick to the east-side galleries and arcades to get a flavour of what the neighbourhood must once have been like. Two of the most intriguing buildings are the 1920s-era William-Marx-Haus, and the Jugendstil Kaufhaus, which remains interesting despite an unsuccessful restoration of the interior.

A trip away from the street will bring you to the city's main park and favoured playground, the Hofgarten. This green space once served as the private park of the Electors Palatine and was strictly off limits to locals. Now, it serves as one of the few places close to the city centre where you can indulge in a spot of getting back to nature. During the summer months, the trails are packed with romancing couples, families and business types eager for a spot of sun and greenery. A nice place to go if you need to get away from the modernism and buzz that makes this city so great.

SIGHTS & ATTRACTIONS

Hofgarten
Düsseldorf doesn't have a lot of parkland. Green spaces, after all, aren't important in a city devoted to the art of making money. The Hofgarten is the main exception to this rule, offering parkland to those in need of some space and calm. Take a stroll through the sculpture garden, which features depictions of such famous locals as the composer Robert Schumann, poet Heinrich Heine and many more.

ⓐ Hofgarten ⏱ 24 hrs Ⓝ U-Bahn: Tonhalle

Schloss Jägerhof
You can't miss this palatial flight of fancy because it is painted a most vivid pink. Examples of fine rococo are few following the destruction caused by World War II, but luckily this whimsical structure survived. Today, the structure houses the Goethe-Museum (see page 96).

ⓐ Jacobistrasse 2 ☎ 899 6262 ⏱ 11.00–17.00 Tues–Fri & Sun, 13.00–17.00 Sat Ⓝ Tram: 704, 707; Bus: 722, 800. Admission charge

Düsseldorf Airport

Kunstmuseum Düsseldorf/
Museum Kunst Palast

	U-Bahn Stop
	Information
	Police Station
	Airport
	Railway Stn
	Bus Station
	Hospital

INSEL STRASSE

STERN STR

PEMPELFORT

ROSEN STR

KAISER STRASSE

JOSEF

BEUYS

OEDERALLEE

Tonhalle

HOFGARTEN

OBERKASSELER BRÜCKE

UFER

Tonhalle/
Ehrenhof

Hofgarten

RAMPE

FRITZ

ROEBER

STRASSE

MAXIMILIAN WEYHE ALLEE

EISKELLER STR

WIMMER

STR

HILARIUS
GILGES-
PLATZ

Theater
Museum

HOFGARTEN STR

Landskrone

RATINGER

STRASSE

PAUL KLEE
PLATZ

NEUBRÜCK

H

HEINE

JAN WELLE
PLATZ

Rhein

RHEINUFER TUNNEL

REUTERKASERNE

RITTER

ALTSTADT

ALTESTADT

STIFTS
PLATZ

ALTSTADT

Kunstsammlung

GRABBE
PLATZ

Deutsche Oper
am Rhein

Schlossturm

SCHLOSSER GASSE

BURG
PLATZ

MÜHLEN

WIMMER G

MERTENS G

Kunsthalle
Düsseldorf

L ZIMMERMANN
STR

CORNELIUS
PLATZ

Akademie
Galerie

KURZE STR

ANDREA STR

STRASSE

ELBERFELDER STR

Rathaus

MARKT
PLATZ

DOLKER

CAPUZINER

STR

H Heine Alle

SCHADOW-
PLATZ

ZOLL STR

MARKT STR

MITTEL

STRASSE

THEODOR KÖRNER STR

SCHADOW

BLUMENSTR

FLINGER

BERGER STR

H Heine
PLATZ

Film
Museum

ACKERMANN STR

WALL STR

GRABEN

KÖNIG STRASSE

Hetjens Museum

SCHULSTR

HAFEN STR

KASERNEN

BREITE

KÖNIGSALLEE

Justiz Min

CARLS-
PLATZ

Steinstrasse/
Königsallee

RHEINUFER TUNNEL

BÄCKER STR

GITSCHEL STR

POST STR

BENRATHER

Heinrich Heine
Institut

BILKER

HOHE

STRASSE

STEIN STR

KÖNIGSALLEE

BERGER ALLEE

Spees
Graben

BASTION

STRASSE

STRASSE

STRASSE

STRASSE

GRÜNSTRASSE

KÖNIGSALLEE

KARLSTADT

SÜD STR

STRASSE

KARL THEODOR STR

BAHN STR

N

HAROLD STRASSE

GRAF ADOLF STR

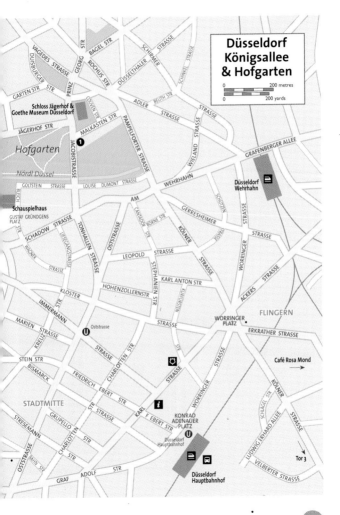

Düsseldorf
Königsallee
& Hofgarten

0   200 metres
0   200 yards

CULTURE

Goethe-Museum Düsseldorf

Everything you could possibly want to know about Goethe can be found at this private museum sponsored by the Anton & Katharina Kippenberg Foundation. Over 35,000 items are owned by the institution, although not all items are on display at one time. If Goethe ever touched it, owned it, wanted it or wrote about it, then it's probably somewhere inside this place. Many of the writer's poems can be seen in their original drafts. Temporary exhibits focus on political and social influences that affected Goethe's works.

ⓐ Schloss Jägerhof, Jacobistrasse 2 ⓣ 899 626 ⓛ 11.00–17.00 Tues–Fri & Sun, 13.00–17.00 Sat ⓝ Tram: 704, 707; Bus: 722, 800. Admission charge

⬥ *In the pink: Schloss Jägerhof*

Museum Kunst Palast (Kunstmuseum Düsseldorf)

For the broadest range of works featuring paintings from some of Europe's biggest names, this is the one-stop-shop to head for. The collection includes works from both German and Dutch masters dating from the Middle Ages to the present day. Especially strong are the exhibits of prints and drawings – the museum owns over 80,000 examples of such work. Also of note are the ceramics, textiles and Asian bronzes. Definitely the best cross-section collection of finds in the city.

ⓐ Ehrenhof 5 ⓣ 899 2460 ⓛ 11.00–18.00 Tues–Sun ⓝ Tram: 701, 706, 711, 715. Admission charge

Theatermuseum

An eclectic collection of pieces related to the vibrant theatre scene that exists in Düsseldorf. Take a peek at locally produced marionettes, toy theatres, old programmes and artefacts once used by some of the biggest stars of the German stage.

ⓐ Jägerhof Strasse 1 ⓣ 899 6130 ⓛ 11.00–17.00 Tues–Sun
ⓝ Tram: 701, 706, 711, 715. Admission charge

RETAIL THERAPY

Shopping is the *raison d'être* of Königsallee. A day out for a discerning socialite isn't considered complete without a stroll along the elegant street – especially if it involves browsing in the boutiques on the swanky east side of the avenue.

Two shopping centres, the **Kö Galerie** (ⓐ Königsallee 60) and **Kö Center** (ⓐ Königsallee 30) are packed with luxurious purveyors of fine goods. Alternatively, the new Schadow Arcade, at the end of the Kö off Schadowplatz, beckons many to its more reasonable selection of high-street chains.

Bogner Shop Look great on the slopes of St Moritz or while practising for Wimbledon by shopping at this high-end sportswear emporium that features designer fashion names. Not necessarily the most practical togs to wear while breaking a sweat – but at least you'll look good while doing it. ⓐ Königsallee 6–8 ⓣ 134 222 ⓛ 10.00–19.00 Mon–Fri, 10.00–18.00 Sat ⓝ U-Bahn: Königsallee

Chanel Everyone knows the name. This branch of the French fashion house contains the full line of offerings, including clothing, accessories, fragrances and cosmetics. ⓐ Kö Center, Königsallee 30 ⓣ 325 935 ⓛ 10.00–20.00 Mon–Sat ⓝ U-Bahn: Königsallee

Etienne Aigner Beautiful European-made accessories, luggage and footwear. A favourite with old-money who don't need flash and dazzle to impress. ⓐ Kö Galerie, Königsallee 60 ⓣ 323 0955 ⓛ 10.00–20.00 Mon–Sat ⓝ U-Bahn: Königsallee

Georg Jensen Scandinavian cutlery and tableware. Very modern. Very sleek. Very expensive. ⓐ Kö Galerie, Königsallee 60 ⓣ 324 281 ⓛ 10.00–20.00 ⓝ U-Bahn: Königsallee

Louis Vuitton Hankering after LV-emblazoned luggage? Well, here is where to find it. ⓐ Kö Center, Königsallee 30 ⓣ 323 230 ⓛ 10.00–20.00 Mon–Sat ⓝ U-Bahn: Königsallee

Ritterskamp Unisex high-fashion boutique offering American, Japanese, British and Italian big names. If you can't find it on the Königsallee, then chances are you'll find it here.
ⓐ Trinkausstrasse 7 ❶ 329 994 ❶ 10.00–18.30 Mon–Fri, 10.00–14.00 Sat ⓝ U-Bahn: Königsallee

Walter Steiger Schuhe Gorgeous footwear from the master of German shoemaking. Styles are beautiful, but tend to focus more on quality and craftsmanship than on temporary trends or fads. ⓐ Kö Galerie, Königsallee 60 ❶ 134 104 ❶ 10.00–20.00 Mon–Sat ⓝ U-Bahn: Königsallee

Wempe Juwelier The finest Swiss watches and high-end designer jewellery. Don't expect any bargains – just good taste.
ⓐ Königsallee 14 ❶ 327 287 ❶ 10.00–19.00 Mon–Fri, 10.00–18.00 Sat ⓝ U-Bahn: Königsallee

AFTER DARK

Restaurants

Malkasten £–££ ❶ Colourful, design-friendly restaurant specialising in French, German and Italian delicacies. The media crowd loves this place as it's one of the only neutral territories where they can mix and mingle with members of the art scene.
ⓐ Jacobistrasse 6 ❶ 173 040 ❶ 12.00–14.30, 18.30–24.00 Mon–Fri, 18.30–24.00 Sat ⓝ Tram: 707; Bus: 752, 754, 755

Victorian Restaurant £££ ❷ Düsseldorf's most exclusive restaurant is an elegant combination of exquisite interiors that provides a perfect backdrop to the modern, international cuisine. Dishes tend to be rich in order to justify the high price tag. Despite this, you need to save room for dessert, which is always the best course of the meal thanks to an inspired pastry team. ⓐ König Strasse 3A ⓣ 865 5020 ⓛ 12.00–14.30, 19.00–24.00 Mon–Sat ⓝ U-Bahn: Königsallee

Bars, clubs & discos

Bei Tino Live piano bar for casual yet elegant evenings. Ask nicely and they may even let you tickle the ivories. ⓐ Königsallee 21 ⓣ 326 463 ⓛ 12.00–03.00 ⓝ U-Bahn: Königsallee

Brauerei Schumacher This is the oldest bar with an on-site brewery in the city. Options are limited by the fact that the place can only serve offerings produced by the larger brewery that owns the establishment. ⓐ Oststrasse 123 ⓣ 326 004 ⓛ 10.00–24.00 ⓝ U-Bahn: Oststrasse

Café Rosa Mond Cologne may be more notorious, but Düsseldorf also has a few gay options if you don't want to make the trek to the other nearby city. This bar/café is the best of the bunch and also has flyers and info on local gay happenings. ⓐ Lierenfelderstrasse 39 ⓣ 992 377 ⓦ www.rosamond.de ⓛ 12.00–24.00; may stay open later on performance and dance evenings – check listings for details ⓝ U-Bahn: Lierenfeld Betriebshof

N.T. Pub Great place for groups due to the large, share-style food platters and pitchers of beer. ⓐ Königsallee 27 ⓣ 138 000 ⓛ 09.00–24.00 Mon–Sat, 09.00–23.00 Sun ⓝ U-Bahn: Königsallee

Sam's West Probably the most popular dance club in town – at least right now. ⓐ Königsallee 52 ⓣ 328 171 ⓛ 20.00–late Ⓝ U-Bahn: Königsallee

Stahlwerk The band Kraftwerk made their name in Düsseldorf, and you can see why with clubs like Stahlwerk as inspiration. Industrial is the theme of this venue. Don't go if you find hard-core techno a turn-off. ⓐ Ronsdorfer Strasse 134 ⓣ 730 8681 ⓦ www.stahlwerk.de ⓛ 20.00–late Fri & Sat Ⓝ U-Bahn: Langenbergerstrasse

Zakk A self-described centre for action, culture and communication, Zakk is the evening locale of choice for poetry, literary readings, performance art and drinking. Go to mix with the bohemian crowd. The beer garden is especially popular during summer evenings. ⓐ Fichtenstrasse 40 ⓣ 973 0010 ⓦ www.zakk.de ⓛ Vary, but box office is usually open from 19.00–23.00 Mon–Sat Ⓝ U-Bahn: Kettwiger Strasse; Bus: 736

Cinemas & theatres
Deutsche Oper am Rhein Fancy a little Andrew Lloyd Webber, or are you mad over Mozart? Then this is the venue to go to. Large-scale mega-musicals and opera from both visiting and top-quality local companies are on the regularly rotating schedule. ⓐ Heinrich Heine Allee 16a ⓣ 890 80 ⓦ www.rheinoper.de ⓛ 10.00–20.00 Mon–Fri, 10.00–18.00 Sat Ⓝ U-Bahn: Heinrich Heine Allee

Robert Schumann Saal Varied schedule of rock, pop and classical performances in addition to art-house cinema, symposiums, lectures and theatre. **ⓐ** Ehrenhof 4 **ⓣ** 899 6211 **ⓦ** www.robert-schumann-saal.de **ⓛ** Vary according to performance schedule **Ⓝ** U-Bahn: Tonhalle

Schauspielhaus This performance venue is the prime place in the city for theatrical entertainment. Expect top comedies and dramas starring the biggest names in Germany. You'll have to know the language if you want to understand the shows because all performances are only presented in German. **ⓐ** Gustaf Gründgens-Platz 1 **ⓣ** 369 911 **ⓦ** www.duesseldorfer-schauspielhaus.de **ⓛ** 11.00–start of performance Mon–Fri, 11.00–13.00 Sat, Sept–June **Ⓝ** U-Bahn: Heinrich Heine Allee

Tonhalle This modern venue houses the world-renowned Düsseldorfer Symphoniker. It may not be the prettiest of locations, but you certainly can't beat the acoustics – or the sounds that come from the amazing musicians who call this place home. **ⓐ** Ehrenhof 2 **ⓣ** 899 6123 **ⓦ** www.tonhalle-duesseldorf.de **ⓛ** 11.00–18.00 Mon–Sat **Ⓝ** U-Bahn: Tonhalle

Tor-3 Big-name musical acts usually choose this renovated factory for large-scale performances. Names that have showcased their talents here include Robbie Williams and Radiohead. On other nights, the place turns into a massive themed dance club. **ⓐ** Ronsdorfer Strasse 134 **ⓣ** 733 6497 **Ⓝ** U-Bahn: Langenbergerstrasse

ⓞ *Cologne is a magnet for tourists*

The suburbs & beyond

Due to the volume of bombs that struck Düsseldorf during World War II, many of its most important historical buildings were destroyed. So a trip to the suburbs away from the Rhine will bring you to pockets of history that escaped the devastating attacks on the city. Benrath with its elegant *Schloss* (castle), Kaiserswerth's atmospheric ruins, and the industrial heritage of Duisburg are all worth escaping Düsseldorf to visit.

BENRATH

South of the city, yet considered a part of Düsseldorf proper, is the town of Benrath. A large *Schloss* (castle) commissioned by and used by the Electors Palatine during the 18th century is the main reason to come to this quiet suburban community. The complex itself is very peaceful, largely due to the synergies between the house and garden. The architect was also a landscape architect and combined the design of both the gardens and *Schloss* together into a complete whole.

Both rococo and neoclassical elements can be witnessed in the completed structure, which is surprisingly intimate in feel, despite its 80-plus rooms. To find out more about the castle, take one of the regular tours that includes stops in the gardens, main reception rooms and private apartments.

GETTING THERE

Take tram 701 or the S-Bahn south to Benrath. Journey time in both cases is approximately 30 minutes.

SIGHTS & ATTRACTIONS

Schloss Benrath

ⓐ Benrather Schlossallee 104 ⓣ 899 3832 ⓒ 10.00–18.00
Tues–Sun, Mar–Oct; 11.00–17.00, Nov–Feb; admission charge
ⓝ Tram: 701 from Jan-Wellem-Platz; S-Bahn: 6 from Düsseldorf
Hauptbahnhof

🔺 The harmonious delights of Benrath castle and gardens

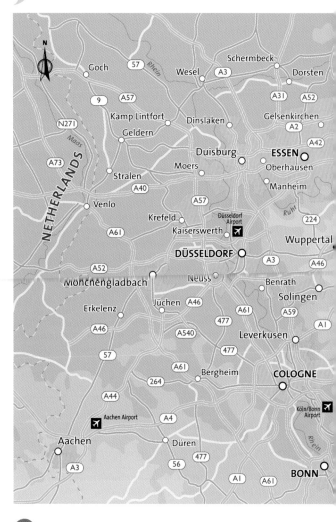

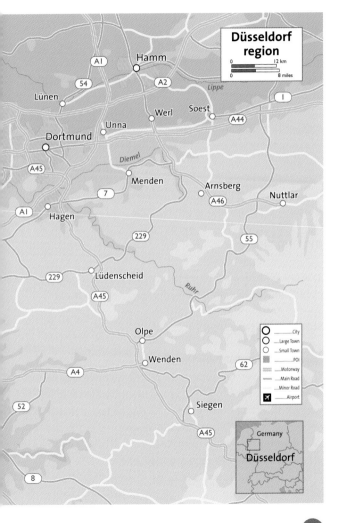

DUISBURG

This industrial town grew rapidly during the years of the Industrial Revolution thanks to its position at the meeting point of the Ruhr and Rhine rivers. While Duisburg is no longer as powerful as it once was, it is still the world's largest inland port. There have been moves by the city government to modernise the town and these initiatives have brought in a clutch of new museums – all for the benefit of tourists like you.

Tourist information ⓐ Duisburg Tourismus, Königstrasse 86 ⓣ 0203 285 440 ⓦ www.duisburg-information.de ⓛ 09.00–18.00 Mon–Fri, 10.00–13.00 Sat

GETTING THERE

Take one of the regular trains that depart from Düsseldorf's Hauptbahnhof. Journey time is approximately 15 minutes.

SIGHTS & ATTRACTIONS

Landschaftspark Duisburg-Nord

The lads will love this converted industrial complex that has been transformed into a miraculous adventure land complete with climbing walls, diving pools and much more. If that doesn't entice, take a stroll through the gardens or drop by the petting zoo for some more sedate activities.

ⓐ Emscherstrasse 71 ⓣ 0203 429 1942 ⓦ www.landschaftspark.de ⓛ 24 hrs

CULTURE

Kultur und Stadthistorisches Museum

This museum is dedicated to telling the history of the city; however, the main reason to come is to look at the exhibits chronicling the life and work of noted geographer and former resident Gerhard Mercator – a man whose contributions you know if you have ever looked at a map. The cartographer was responsible for the creation of the Mercator projection, a system that allowed accurate maps to be drawn on a flat surface. This was a major innovation for sailors who could then plot their courses on a map instead of relying on a compass. Sadly, the descriptions are in German only.

ⓐ Johannes-Corputius-Platz 1 ❶ 0203 283 2640 ⓦ www.stadtmuseum-duisburg.de 🕑 10.00–17.00 Tues– Thur & Sat, 10.00–14.00 Fri, 10.00–18.00 Sun. Admission charge

Museum Küppersmühle

This new museum is dedicated to showcasing contemporary German art, especially works by the well-regarded painter Georg Baselitz. Paintings aren't the only art on display. Conceptual and multi-media offerings also draw the crowds.

ⓐ Philosophenweg 55 ❶ 0203 301 948 ⓦ www.museum-kueppersmuehle.de 🕑 14.00–18.00 Wed, 11.00–18.00 Thur, 11.00–18.00 Sat & Sun. Admission charge

Wilhelm-Lehmbruck-Museum

Fantastic collection of 20th-century sculpture, situated in a quiet city centre park. Combine your visit with a picnic on

a summer day and you have the perfect outdoor artistic adventure.

ⓐ Friedrich-Wilhelm-Strasse 40 **ⓣ** 0203 283 2630
ⓦ www.lehmbruckmuseum.de **ⓛ** 11.00–17.00 Tues–Sat,
10.00–18.00 Sun. Admission charge

TAKING A BREAK

You'll be hard pressed to find a decent place to shop, eat or party in this town. For that, locals go to Düsseldorf, a short 15-minute train journey away. This, after all, is a city all about industry – not culture. When in doubt (or starving) head to the Königstrasse for a bite to eat or drink.

ACCOMMODATION

Youth hostel £ Far from town but good for the price, this hostel offers comfortable beds in a suburban location. **ⓐ** Kalkweg 148
ⓣ 0203 724 164 **ⓝ** Bus: 934, 944

Zum Alten Fritz ££ A convenient location close to the train station makes this hotel a good choice for those looking to explore the town for a longer period. **ⓐ** Klöcknerstrasse 10
ⓣ 0203 351 486

Duisburger Hof £££ The luxury choice in the city but, if you have the option, then stay in Düsseldorf instead. **ⓐ** Neckarstrasse 2
ⓣ 0203 30070 **ⓦ** www.steigenberger.de

KAISERSWERTH

The town of Kaiserswerth was once the most important in the region. Founded in the year 700 as a Benedictine abbey by the monk Suitbertus, it soon prospered, drawing interest from the ruling classes as a potential location for a royal palace.

○ *Ancient ruins at Kaiserswerth speak of its past power*

PINA BAUSCH

In the world of modern dance, choreographer Pina Bausch is considered a major figure. As the director of the Tanztheater Wuppertal Pina Bausch, she has revolutionised movement and its meaning – and her fans flock to this minor industrial town on the outskirts of Düsseldorf to see her works live.

Born in Solingen, Germany, in 1940, Bausch attended ballet class from an early age, eventually ending up at the Folkwang School in Essen, which was under the direction of the renowned choreographer Kurt Jooss.

New York was Bausch's next stop, where she attended Julliard, learning from some of the best in the business, including Limon and Paul Taylor. During her time in the US, Bausch performed for the New American Ballet and Metropolitan Opera ballet company. Yet, ballet failed to inspire her in the way it once did and she began to move in a new direction, away from the conservativism and constraints of classical dance forms. When Bausch accepted the position of director at the Wuppertal Opera Ballet, her career took off. Eventually the company was renamed 'Tanztheater Wuppertal Pina Bausch', acknowledging that her fame had reached global status.

Bausch's works are highly emotional, often revolving around the theme of male–female interaction. A good example of this can be found in the pieces she created for the Spanish film *Talk to Her*, which was directed by Pedro Almodovar. Bausch's large-scale productions combine pathos with humour, often through the use of multi-media, elaborate sets and challenging musical choices.

Expressive dance is now what Bausch is known for; she is credited as the most important force in the development of modern dance in post-war Germany.

So what can you expect from a Bausch performance? Lots of emotion, stamina-testing moves, constant interaction and plenty of raw emotion. Bausch's critics sometimes say that there is little plot in her work or sense of progression, but it has never been her intention to creative a narrative story. Rather, she uses dance to comment and provoke. Bausch wants to unleash feelings and memories or spark emotions – not spin a yarn, using repetition to emphasise her message.

Performances at the Tanztheater Wuppertal Pina Bausch sell out well in advance and should be booked if you want to visit – especially if it coincides with a première. Reduced rates are available for students under the age of 27 with a valid student card.

Tanztheater Wuppertal Pina Bausch

ⓐ Schauspielhaus, Bundesallee 260, Wuppertal-Elberfeld
ⓣ 0202 569 4444 ⓞ 10.00–18.00 Mon–Fri, 10.00–14.00 Sat

GETTING TO WUPPERTAL

Wuppertal is located about 30 km (18$\frac{1}{2}$ miles) east of the city.

You can take one of the regular trains from Düsseldorf's Hauptbahnhof station. The journey time is approximately 30 minutes.

The year 1045 brought the court of the Holy Roman Empire to Kaiserswerth following the construction of the Kaiserpfalz Palace; however, this power was short lived. A year after its completion, the palace was stormed by the Archbishop of Cologne, and the young king of the period, Heinrich IV, was kidnapped. Power never returned to the town and the royal buildings were left to ruin. Any chance of restoring the buildings was destroyed following wars with France and Spain in 1689 and 1702 when the region was bombarded. Little is left of the former splendour, which makes this district of Düsseldorf all the more interesting to explore. Ruins are scattered throughout the area, speaking of a time when an entire region was ruled from within the walls of this town.

British visitors may know the town primarily due to its links with the nurse Florence Nightingale. She learned her trade under the tutelage of a famous deaconess who founded a clinic in the area.

GETTING THERE

Take the U-Bahn 79 line directly to Kaiserswerth from Düsseldorf's Hauptbahnhof station. It will take around 20 minutes.

OBERHAUSEN

Kids getting frantic? Then hop on the train to Oberhausen. This city, located just a few kilometres north of Duisburg, has offerings for both kids and adults and is just a short train or car journey away from Düsseldorf.

GETTING THERE

Take one of the regular trains departing from Hauptbahnhof station for the 30-minute trip, or drive north along the A3 Autobahn and east on the A40 until you reach your destination.

SIGHTS & ATTRACTIONS

CentrO Shopping Centre & Adventure Park

Spend the day shopping at this combination shopping centre and adventure playground. There is a maze and full-size pirate ship next door.

ⓐ Centroallee 1000 ⓣ 0208 456 780 ⓦ www.centro.de
ⓛ Shopping Centre: 10.00–20.00 Mon–Sat; Adventure Park: 10.00–19.00, Apr–Sept; 10.00–19.00 Sat, Sun & school holidays

Gasometer

This former blast furnace now houses international contemporary art. If you suffer from vertigo, you may want to avoid the glass elevator that takes visitors up to the platform 117 m (384 ft) in the air.

ⓐ Am Grafenbusch 90 ⓣ 0208 850 3733 ⓦ www.gasometer.de
ⓛ 10.00–17.00 Tues & Thur–Sun, 10.00–15.00 Wed; audioguides available weekends only. Admission charge

Cologne

The largest city in the region, Cologne is its major tourist attraction too. Principal among its attractions are its position on the Rhine and its majestic cathedral and ancient architecture. Kölsch beer is one of its famous products, as is the perfume, created in the 18th century, known as eau de Cologne.

Tourist Office Köln Tourismus Office ⓐ Unter Fettenhennen 19 ⓣ 0221 221 30400 ⓦ www.koelntourismus.de ⓛ 09.00–21.00 Mon–Sat, 09.00–18.00 Sun, Nov–Apr; 08.00–22.30 Mon–Sat, 09.30–22.00 Sun, May–Oct

GETTING THERE

Take one of the frequent trains from Düsseldorf's Hauptbahnhof to Cologne. The journey time is about 25 minutes. By car, take the A3 Autobahn (see map pages 106–7); however, constant traffic can slow down your trip.

SIGHTS & ATTRACTIONS

Altes Rathaus

The city hall was rebuilt in the 14th century and has a stunning Renaissance exterior. A tower was added in the early 15th century and a loggia in the late 16th century. The loggia was the only part of the building to survive the bombardments of World War II. In front is a glass pyramid housing a Jewish ritual bath: the medieval Jewish quarter was located next to the square.

◒ *The Renaissance façade of the Altes Rathaus*

Cologne cathedral is a must-see Gothic splendour

Gross St Martin

After it was destroyed during World War II, citizens couldn't bear the thought of living without this church, and so it was rebuilt stone by stone. Romanesque in design, its importance to residents lies in the central spire and 13th-century tower, which are considered important landmarks.

ⓐ An Gross St Martin 9 ❶ 0221 164 25650 ❶ 10.15–18.00 Mon–Fri, 10.00–12.30, 13.30–18.00 Sat, 14.00–16.00 Sun
Ⓝ U-Bahn: Heumarkt

Kölner Dom

If you see but one thing in the city, then make it this. A true icon of Cologne, the cathedral is one of the finest examples of Gothic architecture in Europe. Construction took six centuries to complete, due to the massive scale of the project, which was finished in 1880. The two west towers measure 157 m (515 ft) in height and were the tallest structures in the world when completed. The chief purpose behind the design of the cathedral was to hold the relics of the Magi: in order to accommodate the number of pilgrims who wanted to see the remains, a massive building was needed. The relics of the Magi are now kept behind the altar in a beautiful gilt-covered reliquary.

Other attractions are a gigantic oak cross created in the 10th century known as the Gero Cross, and a silver shrine holding the remains of Archbishop Engelbert, murdered in 1225. Combine this with the acres of stained glass, inspiring white statues, filigree choir screens and views from the bell tower, and you have the most unmissable sight in this corner of Germany.

ⓐ Donkloster ⓣ 0221 925 84731 ⓛ 06.00–19.15, except during services; cathedral tower and treasury: 10.00–18.00 Ⓝ U-Bahn: Dom. Admission charge for tower and treasury only

St Gereon

'Breathtaking' is the word that experts in medieval art often use to describe this church which sits on top of a former Roman burial ground. It must have been even more visually stunning during its heyday when gold mosaics covered the walls. Despite this lack of decoration, the structure remains gorgeous.
ⓐ Gereonsdriesch 2–4 ⓣ 0221 134 922 ⓛ 09.00–12.30, 13.30–18.00 Mon–Sat, 13.30–18.00 Sun Ⓝ U-Bahn: Christophestrasse

St Kunibert

The gorgeous stained-glass windows have drawn countless pilgrims to this church for the past seven or more centuries. It is miraculous, considering that the bombs of World War II could so easily have destroyed such beauty. The architecture is late Romanesque, and of the churches near the Rhine, it is certainly the most inspiring. See if you can spot the ancient well under the altar that was once used to help infertile women.
ⓐ Kunibertskloster 2 ⓣ 0221 121 214 ⓛ 09.00–12.00, 15.00–18.00 Ⓝ U-Bahn: Hauptbahnhof

St Maria im Kapitol

This site once housed an opulent Roman temple; however, builders in the 11th century decided to erase the signs of a pagan past by constructing a church, now known as St Maria im Kapitol. The crypt is absolutely massive – the second largest in the nation – but it is the intricately carved, 5-m (16-ft) high doors that impress the most.

ⓐ Marienplatz 19 ⓣ 0221 214 615 ⓛ 09.00–18.00 Mon–Sat, 11.30–17.00 Sun, closed during services ⓝ U-Bahn: Heumarkt

CULTURE

Käthe Kollwitz Museum Köln

Bigger than its sister museum in Berlin, this gallery celebrates the life and works of the famous German graphic artist Käthe Kollwitz. A master at capturing raw human emotion in her works, Kollwitz was the first female artist to be truly fêted in the 20th century.

ⓐ Neu-Markt 18–24, Innenstadt ⓣ 0221 227 2363
ⓦ www.kollwitz.de ⓛ 10.00–18.00 Tues–Fri, 11.00–18.00 Sat & Sun ⓝ The museum is difficult to reach; a taxi journey is recommended. Admission charge

Museum für Angewandte Kunst (Museum of Applied Art)

This museum features an extensive collection of arts and crafts from all over the country dating from the Middle Ages to today.

ⓐ An der Rechtsschule ⓣ 0221 221 33468 ⓛ 11.00–17.00 Tues–Sat; admission charge ⓝ U-Bahn: Hauptbahnhof

Museum Ludwig

Truly one of the best modern art museums in Germany, the Museum Ludwig boasts one of the largest collections of the works of Picasso. Over 700 of the late Spanish artist's pieces were donated by the Ludwig family to the city of Cologne,

promoting the city government to create a museum worthy of their generosity. The bequest in 1976 included some of the artist's most famous works such as *Woman With Artichoke* and *Harlequin With Folded Hands* – two of the most reproduced paintings in the world.

Also on site is the Agfa-Historama, a chronicle of photography over the last 150 years, including examples from some of the greats. The collection of photographs and photographic equipment is considered the largest in the world. ⓐ Bischofsgartenstrasse 1 ① 0221 221 26165 ⓦ www.museenkoeln.de/museum-ludwig ⓛ 10.00–18.00 Tues–Sun, 10.00–23.00 1st Fri of every month ⓝ U-Bahn: Dom. Admission charge

Museum Schnütgen

Religious art is the focus of this impressive museum housed in an actual converted church. The beautiful architecture of the building acts as a wonderful counterpoint to the collection, which features examples of iconography and religious depictions in paint, wood, ivory and weavings. If you like Madonnas of the non-singing variety, then you'll be very happy. ⓐ Cäcilienstrasse 29 ① 0221 221 23620 ⓛ 10.00–17.00 Tues–Fri, 11.00–17.00 Sat & Sun ⓝ U-Bahn: Neumarkt. Admission charge

Römisch-Germanisches Museum (Roman-Germanic Museum)

This museum houses a wonderful collection of Roman finds discovered in the Rhine valley region. The highlight of any tour is the Dionysos-Mosaik dating from the 3rd century AD. The mosaic

was uncovered during the peak of World War II when excavators building a bomb shelter came across the brightly tiled floor.
ⓐ Roncalliplatz 4 ⓣ 0221 221 24438 ⓒ 10.00–17.00 Tues–Sun; admission charge ⓝ U-Bahn: Hauptbahnhof

Wallraf-Richartz Museum/Foundation Corboud

This collection of work was founded in the 19th century and is the oldest public art gallery in the city. The principal attraction in its early days was a series of gothic paintings created by local artists, but the museum has grown much larger since then. Today, it houses works created between 1300 and 1900.

🔺 *Make merry at Cologne's Christmas market*

Big names include Albrecht Dürer, Paul Klee and Max Ernst. In keeping with the museum's roots, there is a strong focus on dark gothic subject matter – so keep the kids away if they are easily spooked. ⓐ Martinstrasse 39 ① 0221 221 21119 ⓛ 10.00–18.00 Wed & Fri, 10.00–18.00 Thur, 11.00–18.00 Sat & Sun ⓝ U-Bahn: Hauptbahnfof. Admission charge

RETAIL THERAPY

A monthly flea market is held in the grounds of the Alter Markt, which is well worth attending if you want to find both kitsch and treasures. Contact the tourist office for further details on anticipated dates and times. Alternatively, get a feel for everyday life by doing a spot of fresh food shopping at the market on Wilhelmsplatz on Saturdays (ⓛ 08.00–14.00 ⓝ U-Bahn: Florastrasse).

Eau de Cologne Yes, the smelly stuff was first produced in these parts. Designed to help make smelly, non-bathing aristocrats less odorous, it may seem a little sweet to modern noses – but it makes a great souvenir for the folks back home. ⓐ Glockengasse 4711 ① 0221 925 0450 ⓛ 09.00–18.00 Mon–Sat ⓝ U-Bahn: Neumarkt

TAKING A BREAK

Fischers Weingenuss und Tafelfreuden £££ ① Relax at this chichi eatery that stocks one of the best ranges of wine in the city – over 40 kinds of which can be bought by the glass. Perfect when you need a touch of relaxation after a long day of sightseeing. ⓐ Hohenstaufenring 53 ⓣ 0221 310 8470 ⓛ 12.00–15.00, 18.00–23.00 Mon–Fri, 18.00–23.00 Sat ⓝ Tram: 12, 16, 18

AFTER DARK

Restaurants

Green Card £ ❷ Due to this establishment's mission to provide 'inexpensive and earthy' food with a Eurasian twist to the masses, the bohemian and artsy crowd love it here. Menu items are seasonally based, using whatever is available at the market that day. ⓐ Neue Maastrichter Strasse 2 ⓣ 0221 89 3725 ⓛ 12.00–15.00, 18.00–23.00 Mon–Sat ⓝ Tram: 6, 15

Hanse Stube £££ ❸ Arguably Cologne's finest restaurant, this French establishment features delightful combinations of tried and true dishes with inspiring new flavours. The fixed-price lunch is a good deal for those who want fine dining without breaking the bank. ⓐ Trankgasse 1–5 ⓣ 0221 2701 ⓛ 12.00–14.30, 18.00–24.00 ⓝ U-Bahn: Hauptbahnhof

Bars, clubs & discos

Alt-Köln am Dom The archetypal beerhall. Gothic interiors, hearty food, jolly patrons and sloshing suds. Go for an hour or go for the night. ⓐ Trankgasse 7–9 ⓣ 0221 137 471 ⓛ 11.00–24.00 ⓝ U-Bahn: Hauptbahnhof

E-Werk Best dance club in town bar none. Sometimes a disco, sometimes a concert venue. You'll be pleased either way.

Schanzenstrasse 28 0221 962 7910 22.00–late Fri & Sat
U-Bahn: Keupstrasse

Cinemas & theatres
Oper der Städt Köln The place to hear opera in the Rhineland. Performances feature some of the biggest names in the industry. Book well in advance. Offenbachplatz 0221 221 8248 09.00–18.00 Mon–Fri, 09.00–14.00 Sat U-Bahn: Neumarkt

ACCOMMODATION

Brandenburger Hof £–££ Great family-run establishment with warm interiors and a filling breakfast included in the rate. Just three blocks from the river and a few steps from the cathedral. Brandenburgerstrasse 2–4 0221 122 889 U-Bahn: Hauptbahnhof

Excelsior Hotel Ernst £££ For years this hotel has been the address of choice in Cologne. Built in 1863, there is an opulent 'old world' feel, right down to the original Anthony Van Dyck hanging on its walls. It may not feature the same levels of service and modernity as the rival Hyatt Regency – but who needs an anonymous chain when you can get this slice of luxury? Trankgasse 1–5 0221 270 3333
www.excelsiorhotelernst.de U-Bahn: Hauptbahnhof

The sleek lines of Düsseldorf airport

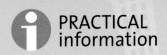

Directory

GETTING THERE

By air

The most convenient entry point for scheduled flights from the UK is Düsseldorf International Airport. Reconstructed in 2003, it is one of the most modern airports in the country, accessible by both scheduled and low-cost airlines. Depending on traffic, a taxi will cost about €20 and take approximately 15 minutes to reach the Altstadt. Those on a budget can take the S1 or S7 bus from the airport to the city centre for around €2. Buses depart every few minutes. Köln/Bonn International Airport is another arrival option, located approximately 60 minutes away by car – although few long-haul carriers service this destination. Those flying Ryanair will arrive at Niederrhein Airport, close to the Dutch border, around 50 km (31 miles) west of the city. Shuttle buses depart for Düsseldorf's main train station shortly after arrival. The journey currently costs €16 and takes an hour. See pages 48, 52–3 for more details on airports.

Many people are aware that air travel emits CO_2, which contributes to climate change. You may be interested in the possibility of lessening the environmental impact of your flight through the charity Climate Care, which offsets your CO_2 by funding environmental projects around the world. Visit ⓦ www.climatecare.org

By rail

Though travelling by rail is often a more expensive option than flying from the UK, it at least allows you the chance to see something of the countryside en route. The most common routes by rail cut through Belgium via Eurostar, with a change at Brussels.

The total journey time is approximately 5–6 hours depending on connections. The monthly *Thomas Cook European Rail Timetable* has up-to-date schedules for European international and domestic train services.

Eurostar ⓘ Reservations (UK): 08705 186 186

ⓦ www.eurostar.com

Thomas Cook European Rail Timetable ⓘ UK: 01733 416 477, USA: 1 800 322 3834 ⓦ www.thomascookpublishing.com

By car

The German motorway system is well integrated into the European motorway network. The easiest route to take from the UK will bring you to Calais by ferry, up into Belgium past Bruges and Ghent, through Antwerp to Eindhoven and then along the A61 straight to the city. The journey time is approximately 7–8 hours.

Driving in Düsseldorf is a breeze when compared to other busy cities. While World War II may have levelled most of the city, it also allowed town planners to create broad multi-lane avenues. Congestion issues outside of the traditional rush hours are few.

By bus

Long-distance buses connect Düsseldorf with most other European countries (ⓦ www.eurolines.com). Travellers may have to change buses in Brussels to reach their final destination. The arrival point is at the bus station on Worringer Strasse. From London by National Express, the fastest journey time is approximately 13–14 hours, depending on connections.

ENTRY FORMALITIES
Documentation

Visitors to Germany who are citizens of the UK, Ireland, Australia, the US, Canada or New Zealand will need a passport but not a visa for stays of up to three months. South African nationals do require a visa. If you are travelling from other countries, you may need a visa and it is best to check before you leave home.

Customs

There are no customs controls at borders for visitors from EU countries. Visitors from EU countries can bring in, or take out, goods without restrictions on quantity or value, as long as these goods are for personal use only. Visitors from outside the EU are subject to the following restrictions.

Most personal effects and the following items are duty-free: a portable typewriter, one video camera or two still cameras with ten rolls of film each, a portable radio, a tape recorder and a laptop computer provided they show signs of use; 400 cigarettes or 50 cigars or 250 g of tobacco; 2 litres of wine or 1 litre of liquor per person over 17 years old; fishing gear; one bicycle; skis; tennis or squash racquets; and golf clubs.

As entry requirements and customs regulations are subject to change, you should always check the current situation with your local travel agent, airline or a German embassy or consulate before you leave.

MONEY

The currency in Germany is the euro. A euro is divided into 100 cents. Currency denominations are: 50 euro, 20 euro, 10 euro,

5 euro, 2 euro, 1 euro, 50 cents, 20 cents, 10 cents, 5 cents and 1 cent. You can withdraw money using ATMs at many German banks.

The most widely accepted credit card is Mastercard. American Express and Visa are less commonly permitted. Many smaller businesses, including some restaurants, taverns, smaller hotels and most market stalls do not accept credit card payment. This is especially true outside the city and the main tourist destinations. It is advisable to always carry a small amount of cash to cover your day's purchases.

HEALTH, SAFETY & CRIME

It is not necessary to take any special health precautions while travelling in Germany. Tap water is safe to drink, but do not drink any water from surrounding lakes or rivers. Many Germans prefer bottled mineral water (*Mineralwasser*).

If you are going to do a lot of walking in forested areas, it is necessary to be careful of ticks. These blood-sucking parasites can transmit dangerous viral infections, along with various bacterial diseases. A good deterrent is the insecticide peremethrin sprinkled over your clothes. It is also wise to avoid walking through long grass with bare legs. In any case, after a walk always check your body for ticks. If you find one, remove it immediately with a pair of tick tweezers (*Zeckenzange*). These can be bought at pharmacies. Ask how to use them when buying. If a rash develops from a bite, consult a doctor immediately.

Pharmacies (or *Apotheken*) are marked by a large green cross or red 'A' outside the front door. German pharmacists are always well stocked and staff can provide expert advice.

German health care is of a good standard, but it is not free. In most cases your travel insurance should provide the coverage you need.

As in any other big cities, crime is a fact of life in Düsseldorf. Petty theft (bag-snatching, pick-pocketing) is the most common form of trouble for tourists; however, you are unlikely to experience violence or assault. Never leave valuables on view in your car, and always lock it. Strolling around the inner city at night is fairly safe, but avoid dimly lit streets. Particular areas to avoid are Hauptbahnhof, Worringer Platz and the city parks after dark. Your hotel will warn you about any other areas to avoid.

When using public transport or walking on the street, carry your wallet in your front pocket, keep bags closed at all times, never leave valuables on the ground when you are seated at a table, and always wear camera bags and purses crossed over your chest. For details of emergency numbers, refer to the 'Emergencies' section on page 138.

OPENING HOURS

Most businesses open 09.00–18.30 Monday–Friday. Retail shops sometimes stay open until 20.00 on Thursdays. On Saturdays, smaller boutiques will close at 14.00, while larger department stores and chains extend hours to 20.00. Stores generally do not open on Sundays or public holidays. Banks open 08.00–13.00, 14.00–16.00 Monday–Friday (until 15.30 on Thursdays). Cultural institutions close for one day a week – usually Mondays.

Standard hours are 09.00–18.00. Only the biggest and most popular sights remain open seven days a week.

Usual post office opening hours are 08.00–18.00 Mondays–Fridays and 08.00–12.00 Saturdays.

TOILETS

At airports, railway stations, U-Bahn and S-Bahn stations, you should not have a problem finding toilets. Most locals, when pressed, resort to using facilities at cafés, restaurants and bars, though using them may not be appreciated if you are not a customer.

The cleanest public toilets are those with an attendant, who will expect a small tip. Another good bet is the toilets at museums. Women's toilets are often marked with the usual

⬤ Post boxes are easy to spot

pictograms, but if not, an 'F' is for *Frauen* (Ladies), and an 'H' means *Herren* (Gentlemen).

CHILDREN

Germany is generally a child-friendly place and no special health precautions need be taken for children. Most restaurants welcome children, and some even have play corners or outdoor playgrounds for the kids. There is usually a children's menu with portions to go with the normal menu and, if you ask, the staff will often be able to supply your children with pencils and paper at the table.

Nappies and other baby articles are readily obtained from supermarkets, *Apotheken* (pharmacies) or a *Drogerie* – like a drugstore selling various articles, but without prescription medications. Things to see and do with the children while in town include:

Altstadt The little ones will love the cobbled lanes and atmospheric squares of the city's Old Town. Go in summer when the squares come alive with street performers and buskers.

Grosses Schützenfest (Riflemen's Meeting) This eight-day celebration is held on the banks of the Rhine in late July every year. Children will adore the rides, games and Ferris wheel – in addition to the local tradition of cartwheeling practised by local boys all over the streets of the Altstadt.

Hofgarten Park Let them run free in the city's favourite green space. Live music often adds to the fun.

COMMUNICATIONS

Phones

Coin-operated public phones are rare; card-operated phones are far more common. Telephone cards (*Telefonkarten*) can be bought at any post office and at some shops such as bookshops or kiosks at railway stations. A display shows how much credit is left. Instructions on how to use public telephones are written in English in phone booths for international calls. Otherwise, lift up the receiver, insert the telephone card and dial the number.

When making an international call, dial the international code you require and drop the initial zero of the area code you are ringing. The international dialling code for calls from Germany to Australia is 0061, to the Irish Republic 00353, to South Africa 0027, to New Zealand 0064, to the UK 0044, and to the US and Canada 001.

The code for dialling Germany from abroad, after the access code (00 in most countries) is 49. To call Düsseldorf from within Germany, dial 0211 and then the number, unless calling within the city itself when there is no need to dial 0211.

Post

Postal services are quick and efficient. There are many post offices throughout the city, but the main branch is located on Konrad-Adenauer-Platz. Stamps can be bought at the post offices or from automatic vending machines outside post offices. Post boxes are yellow.

Internet

Internet access is provided by some libraries and internet cafés around the city. Two convenient locations are:

G@rden ⓐ Rathausufer 8 ⓣ 866 160 ⓛ 11.00–01.00

Surf Inn ⓐ 3rd Floor, Galeria Kaufhof, Königsallee 1–9 ⓣ 139 1213 ⓛ 09.30–20.00

ELECTRICITY

The standard electrical current is 220 volts. Two-pin adaptors can be purchased at most electrical shops.

TRAVELLERS WITH DISABILITIES

Facilities for visitors with disabilities are generally quite good in Germany. These facilities are usually indicated by a blue pictogram of a person in a wheelchair. In all towns and cities there are reserved car parks for people in wheelchairs, and motorway service stops, airports and main railway stations always have suitable toilet facilities. Most trains also have toilets accessible for wheelchairs. Furthermore, many cinemas, theatres, museums and public buildings are accessible. Many of Düsseldorf's hotels are wheelchair-friendly; however, you will need to make a request when you book. For further advice on facilities in Düsseldorf contact the tourist office (see page 137).

Facilities for visitors with disabilities arriving at the city's main international airports are good, though travellers with special needs should inform their airlines in advance.

A useful source of advice when in Germany is **NatKo e.V.** ⓐ Kötherhofstrasse Mainz 4 ⓣ 01631 250 410. Useful websites include:

Ⓦ www.sath.org (US-based site)

Ⓦ www.access-able.com (general advice on worldwide travel)

FURTHER INFORMATION

Tourist offices

There are three branches of the Düsseldorf tourist office. All provide maps and information in English.

Tourist Office Altstadt ⓐ Burgplatz ☎ 602 5753 🕐 12.00–18.00

Tourist Office Finanzkaufhaus ⓐ Berliner Allee 33 ☎ 300 4897 🕐 10.00–18.00 Mon–Sat

Tourist Office Hauptbahnhof ⓐ Immermannstrasse 65b ☎ 172 0222 🕐 10.00–18.00 Mon–Sat

BACKGROUND READING

Düsseldorf by Angela Pfotenhauer (Greven, 2002). Good coffee-table pictorial guide to the city.

Glass Art Reflecting the Centuries: Masterpieces from the Glasmuseum Hentreich in Museum Kunst Palast Düsseldorf by Helmut Riche (Prestel Publishing, 2002). Beautiful guide to the extensive glass collection of one of the city's best museums.

Heinrich Heine edited by David Cram and T J Reed (Phoenix Press, 1997). Romantic poetry from the pen of Düsseldorf's favourite scribe.

Emergencies

EMERGENCY NUMBERS

In an emergency call:

Ambulance 112 **Fire brigade** 112 **Police** 110

MEDICAL SERVICES

The British Embassy has a list of English-speaking doctors and dentists. However, most doctors in Düsseldorf speak at least the English basics. Make sure that you have a European Health Insurance Card (if you are from the EU) and/or private travel insurance. For serious emergencies, go directly to the emergency departments of the main public hospital in town (see below).

Emergency pharmacy

Pharmacies (or *Apotheken*) are marked by a green cross or red 'A' outside the front door. A list of pharmacies open in the evenings and on Sundays should be displayed near the pharmacy door.

EMERGENCY PHRASES

Help! Hilfe! *Heelfe!*   **Fire!** Feuer! *Foyer!*   **Stop!** Halt! *Halt!*

Call an ambulance/a doctor/the police/the fire service!
Rufen Sie bitte einen Krankenwagen/einen Arzt/die Polizei/
die Feuerwehr!
*Roofen zee bitter inen krankenvaagen/inen artst/dee
politsye/dee foyervair!*

Hospitals

Marien Hospital Düsseldorf ⓐ Rochusstrasse 2 ⓣ 44 000
ⓦ www.marien-hospital.de

Police

You are unlikely to come into contact with the police unless you are the victim of a crime. The central police station is located at:
Central police station ⓐ Ulmenstrasse ⓣ 870 9230

Lost property

If you lose or have anything stolen, go straight to the police. For details, look in the Yellow Pages (*Gelbe Seiten*) under *Polizei*. Otherwise, call municipal lost and found number on ⓣ 899 3285.

EMBASSIES & CONSULATES

Australian Embassy ⓐ Wallstrasse 76–79, Berlin ⓣ 030 880 0880 ⓛ 08.30–13.00, 14.00–17.00 Mon–Thur, 08.30–16.15 Fri
British Consulate ⓐ Yorckstrasse 19 ⓣ 94480 ⓛ 09.00–11.00, 12.00–16.00 Mon–Fri
Canadian Consulate ⓐ Benratherstrasse 8 ⓣ 172 170 ⓛ 08.30–17.30 Mon–Fri
Irish Embassy ⓐ Friedrichstrasse 200, Berlin ⓣ 030 220 720 ⓛ 09.30–12.30, 14.30–16.45 Mon–Fri
New Zealand Embassy ⓐ Friedrichstrasse 60, Berlin ⓣ 030 206 210 ⓛ 09.00–13.00, 14.00–17.30 Mon–Thur, 09.00–13.00, 14.00–16.30 Fri
Republic of South Africa Embassy ⓐ Tiergartenstrasse 18, Berlin ⓣ 030 220 730 ⓛ 08.00–12.45, 13.30–16.30 Mon–Fri
US Consulate ⓐ Willi-Becker-Allee 10 ⓣ 788 8927 ⓛ 09.00–17.00

INDEX

SPOT A CITY IN SECONDS

This great range of pocket city guides will have you in the know in no time. Lightweight and packed with detail on the most important things from shopping and sights to non-stop nightlife, they knock spots off chunkier, clunkier versions. Titles include:

Amsterdam	Bratislava	Glasgow	Madrid	Salzburg
Antwerp	Bruges	Gothenburg	Marrakech	Sarajevo
Athens	Brussels	Granada	Milan	Seville
Barcelona	Bucharest	Hamburg	Monte Carlo	Sofia
Belfast	Budapest	Hanover	Munich	Stockholm
Belgrade	Cardiff	Helsinki	Naples	Strasbourg
Berlin	Cologne	Hong Kong	New York	St Petersburg
Bilbao	Copenhagen	Istanbul	Nice	Tallinn
Bologna	Cork	Kiev	Oslo	Turin
	Dubai	Krakow	Palermo	Valencia
	Dublin	Leipzig	Palma	Venice
	Dubrovnik	Lille	Paris	Verona
	Dusseldorf	Lisbon	Prague	Vienna
	Edinburgh	Ljubljana	Porto	Vilnius
	Florence	London	Reykjavik	Warsaw
	Frankfurt	Lyon	Riga	Zagreb
	Gdansk		Rome	Zurich
	Geneva			
	Genoa			

HAMBURG VILNIUS BILBAO NEW YORK GLASGOW

Available from all good bookshops, your local Thomas Cook travel store or browse and buy on-line at www.thomascookpublishing.com

Thomas Cook Publishing

The publishers would like to thank the following individuals and organisations for providing their copyright photographs for this book: Düsseldorf Marketing & Tourismus GmbH pages 7, 11, 15, 21, 28, 43, 66, 105; Ulrich Otte – Düsseldorf Marketing & Tourismus GmbH pages 52, 64; World Pictures/Photoshot pages 9, 19, 23, 78, 91; Pictures Colour Library page 123; all the rest Christopher Holt Ltd.

Copy editor: Joanne Osborne
Proofreader: Ian Faulkner

Send your thoughts to
books@thomascook.com

- **Found a great bar, club, shop or must-see sight that we don't feature?**

- **Like to tip us off about any information that needs updating?**

- **Want to tell us what you love about this handy little guidebook and more importantly how we can make it even handier?**

Then here's your chance to tell all! Send us ideas, discoveries and recommendations today and then look out for your valuable input in the next edition of this title. As an extra 'thank you' from Thomas Cook Publishing, you'll be automatically entered into our exciting prize draw.

Send an email to the above address (stating the book's title) or write to: CitySpots Project Editor, Thomas Cook Publishing, PO Box 227, The Thomas Cook Business Park, Unit 18, Coningsby Road, Peterborough PE3 8SB, UK.